The Wellbeing Workout

Rick Hughes • Andrew Kinder
Cary L. Cooper

The Wellbeing Workout

How to manage stress and develop resilience

Rick Hughes
Aberdeen, UK

Andrew Kinder
London, UK

Cary L. Cooper
Manchester Business School
University of Manchester
Manchester, UK

ISBN 978-3-319-92551-6   ISBN 978-3-319-92552-3 (eBook)
https://doi.org/10.1007/978-3-319-92552-3

Library of Congress Control Number: 2018952934

© The Editor(s) (if applicable) and The Author(s), under exclusive licence to Springer International Publishing AG, part of Springer Nature 2019
This work is subject to copyright. All rights are solely and exclusively licensed by the Publisher, whether the whole or part of the material is concerned, specifically the rights of translation, reprinting, reuse of illustrations, recitation, broadcasting, reproduction on microfilms or in any other physical way, and transmission or information storage and retrieval, electronic adaptation, computer software, or by similar or dissimilar methodology now known or hereafter developed.
The use of general descriptive names, registered names, trademarks, service marks, etc. in this publication does not imply, even in the absence of a specific statement, that such names are exempt from the relevant protective laws and regulations and therefore free for general use.
The publisher, the authors and the editors are safe to assume that the advice and information in this book are believed to be true and accurate at the date of publication. Neither the publisher nor the authors or the editors give a warranty, express or implied, with respect to the material contained herein or for any errors or omissions that may have been made. The publisher remains neutral with regard to jurisdictional claims in published maps and institutional affiliations.

This Palgrave Macmillan imprint is published by the registered company Springer Nature Switzerland AG
The registered company address is: Gewerbestrasse 11, 6330 Cham, Switzerland

Rick: To Kirsty.
Andrew: To Jane, Hannah, Isabel and Lydia.
Cary: To Jai, Isabella, Emme, Skyla, Bodhi and Amabel—my wonderful grandchildren.

Foreword

We live in fast changing times and for many of us over recent years work intensity has been steadily increasing. We seem to work harder and live in a world where we are always on, always in contact, which might be great for us socially but is more difficult to manage effectively in the context of work. And whilst we may be working harder, financial security is not improving for many as average wages have stagnated over the last decade. Furthermore, job security itself is reducing as jobs change, and as more people work as self-employed or in the gig economy. Added to that is a more unpredictable economy and future as we see a different era of geo-politics and a future more than ever driven by advances in technology.

This changing world of work has clearly also created many new opportunities for work, and greater flexibility, and these new ways of working have helped to sustain the almost record levels of employment we see today. But the combined effect of work intensity and more uncertainty and insecurity can't ultimately be sustainable or good for us.

The evidence is there and growing. CIPD research has shown that stress is the biggest source of absenteeism, and many surveys on physical and mental health issues are showing how much these are growing as part of modern society. It is good to see the UK Government and many others raising awareness and challenging us all to address wellbeing issues both in our workplaces and in wider society.

The trend of work, organisations, and management practice over the last 30 or 40 years has been significantly driven by mantras of efficiency, of standardisation, and cultures of rules and command and control. This is undoubtedly beginning to change and not before time. We have to put people back at the heart of our thinking, and particularly recognise that helping to get the best out of them is a lot about understanding and supporting their wellbeing.

And we have to think more about the whole person, the individual, not just that element that might turn up at work. Our wellbeing is a combination of work, home and the rest of our lives and we can't just compartmentalise. Yet working culture has been one that has typically sought to ignore those other parts of our lives. Even talking about issues at home that might impact our performance at work has usually been off limits, both for the individual and for their managers.

The agenda is big. We have recognised more and more that we need to create better work, or more 'good' work, where people have more of a say in what they do, can see opportunities to develop and grow and that we use their skills and talents effectively. Our recent survey on UK Working Lives showed clearly the importance of attributes of work that help to sustain a better sense of wellbeing, which in turn leads to more engagement and productivity.

We have to teach managers much more about understanding the wellbeing of their teams and how they can impact it. Many of these skills are the so-called 'soft' skills such as listening skills, coaching and support. In turn we have to help people understand their own wellbeing, how to adjust and how to cope better with stress and the inevitable ups and downs, and to develop more resilience. We must also work harder to create working cultures that are less stressful, that support more flexible working, that don't create cultures of fear but are supportive and inclusive.

This book offers a hugely rich source of insight and very practical guidance on these and many other aspects of wellbeing. Aristotle long ago observed that the outcome of humanity and civilisation should be greater contentment or wellbeing, what he called eudemonia. That idea has been echoed by philosophers, and sometimes politicians as well, over the ages. Now is the time for us all to get more serious about it.

CEO Chartered Institute of Personnel and Peter Cheese
Development (CIPD), London, UK

Preface

Wellbeing encompasses a multi-dimensional matrix of our self and our world: the physical, emotional, psychological, spiritual, philosophical, social, cultural and relational. Added to this, we're all individuals, so this weaves together to create our own unique, and beautiful, tartan tapestry of personality and identity.

We might clamour for peace, calm and tranquillity but more often than not, we live in a furiously fast and frenetic environment, punctuated by demands from others as we muscle through life. We seek control but realise we live in a world of chaos.

What we want is often what we don't need; we want instant gratification but need delayed gratification. We want achievement today but need to work for it. We want to win but need to embrace coming second. We want loyalty and trust but need to earn it. We want to blame but need to forgive.

Nothing stays still. Change becomes the only constant. Life cycle events come and go and we will suffer the slings and arrows of relationship, family, work and wider crisis misfortunes.

Life isn't always pretty or easy or happy or positive but it can become prettier, easier, happier and more positive. That's where stress management and resilience comes in.

If we can learn to identify the causes, consequences and cures of our stress and, at the same time, learn how to become more adaptive and accepting of life's ups and downs, then we're going to be pretty resourceful and robust and better able to support others.

Wellbeing involves recognising the importance of building up and maintaining the mental health of ourselves and those close to us. Meeting the tough times head on, dealing with them, getting through them and emerging out the other side will also enable us to enjoy the beautiful things in life, allowing us to better appreciate the triumphs, the joys, the achievements, the successes and the things which make us truly happy.

We hope this book helps you to nourish and enhance your own wellbeing.

Aberdeen, UK Rick Hughes
London, UK Andrew Kinder
Manchester, UK Cary L. Cooper

Acknowledgements

This book is dedicated to the hundreds of organisations and thousands of clients the authors have had the pleasure of working with over many years.

It is through them that the authors have learned to better understand the many issues that impact wellbeing, through effective stress management and resilience strategies. This book is a culmination of around 100 years of collective insight and learning from the authors.

Special thanks to Stephen, Gabriel and all the team at Palgrave Macmillan for their support, encouragement and professionalism.

Contents

Section I	Stress Management	1
1	Managing Workload Pressure	3
2	Choice and Control	9
3	Task Prioritisation	15
4	Constructive Criticism and Managing Rejection	21
5	Maximising Personal Efficiency	29
6	Dealing with Difficult People	35
7	Managing Conflict at Home and Work	41
8	Redundancy and Retirement	47

9	Work Satisfaction	53
10	Effective Delegation	59
11	To Know or Not to Know	65
12	How to Get on in Your Career	71
13	Confident Public Speaking	77
14	The Myths of Perfectionism	83
15	Managing Change in Organisations	89
16	Working with Global Uncertainty	93
17	Personal Stress Management Toolkit	99
18	Organisational Savviness	105
19	Networking and Your Dream Team	109
20	Spotting Signs of Stress in Others	115
Section II	Personal and Family Life Management	121
21	Relationship MOT	123
22	When Relationships End	129

23	Anxiety Management	133
24	Living with Depression	139
25	Changing Negative-Thinking Patterns	145
26	Supporting Elderly Dependents	151
27	Bereavement and Loss	157
28	Stages in Life	163
29	Help: Asking for It and Finding It	169
30	Being Childless or Child-Free	175
31	Pregnancy and Birth	181
32	Parenting Pre-teens	187
33	Parenting Teenagers	193
34	When Children Leave Home	199
35	Embracing a Mid-life Crisis	205
36	Addictions	209
37	Being Single	215

38	Personal Wellness Toolkit	221
39	Pain Management	227
40	Coping with Illness	233

Section III	Personal Resilience	241
41	Personal Fulfilment, Satisfaction and Purpose	243
42	Work-Life Balance	249
43	Personal and Professional Development	255
44	Acceptance Strategies	261
45	Emotional Intelligence	267
46	Assertiveness	273
47	Constructive Anger	279
48	Developing Self-confidence	285
49	Setting Meaningful Goals	291
50	Mindfulness	297
51	Life Cycle Events: Losses and Gains	303

52	Rest and Relaxation	309
53	Looking After Yourself and Self-Care	315
54	Problem-Focused Resilience	321
55	Solution-Focused Resilience	327
56	Change-Focused Resilience	333
57	Managing a Crisis	339
58	Avoiding Burnout	345
59	How to Tolerate Ambiguity	351
60	Procrastination	357

| References | 363 |
| Index | 365 |

About the Authors

Rick Hughes has been a wellbeing consultant, workplace counsellor, coach, employee support troubleshooter and writer for more than 22 years providing support, counsel or guidance for thousands of individuals. See www.calma.co.uk

He is Head of Service for the University of Aberdeen Counselling Service, before which he was Lead Advisor: Workplace for the British Association for Counselling and Psychotherapy, editor of *Counselling at Work* Journal, Deputy Chair of the Association for Counselling at Work, Director of Person-Centred Therapy (PCT) Glasgow, Clinical Case Manager, Account Manager and Business Development Consultant at Independent Counselling and Advisory Services (ICAS) and a founding member of the Association for Coaching.

Andrew Kinder is a British Psychological Society Registered Coach and a chartered counselling and occupational psychologist. He was recognised by the British Association for Counselling and Psychotherapy with a fellowship for his contribution to workplace counselling.

He has been published widely, particularly in the areas of work-related stress, trauma and stress management and is currently Clinical Director of a large employee assistance programme (EAP) provider, www.optimahealth.co.uk. He is active as a coaching practitioner with his own caseload of clients. See www.andrewkinder.co.uk

Cary L. Cooper is the author and editor of more than 150 scholarly books and is one of Britain's most quoted business gurus. He is the 50th Anniversary Professor of Organizational Psychology and Health at Manchester Business

School, University of Manchester. He is a founding President of the British Academy of Management, a Companion of the Chartered Management Institute and one of only a few UK Fellows of the (American) Academy of Management, President of the Chartered Institute of Personnel and Development (CIPD), President of the British Academy of Management, President of the Institute of Welfare and former President of RELATE. He was the founding editor of the *Journal of Organizational Behaviour*, former editor of the scholarly journal *Stress and Health* and is the editor-in-chief of the Wiley-Blackwell *Encyclopaedia of Management*, now in its third edition. He was awarded the CBE by the Queen in 2001 for his contributions to occupational health and safety; and in 2014 he was awarded a Knighthood for his contribution to the social sciences.

Section I

Stress Management

1

Managing Workload Pressure

Spotlight

Workload is simply the amount of work we have scheduled with our name on it, through employment, academic demands or domestic pressures. But it's not quite as simple as that. It's rare that we have complete control, management or authority regarding the demands placed upon us.

If it's the right amount of demand on us, then it gives us a reason to get up in the morning, providing a structure and routine. It might help to motivate, inspire and give us purpose and meaning. It might also contribute to our identity and persona, how we see ourselves and how others see us.

But we can also fall prey to a workload that becomes counterproductive, leading to stress and anxiety at one level, or apathy, demotivation and lethargy at the other. We can lose ourselves in our workload bubble, and we could lose sight of the wider picture and the world around us.

In much of what we do, we form a 'psychological contract'. For instance, in exchange for our work, we get rewarded by some benefit, financial remuneration, pay-off or productivity value outcome. If we work in an organisation, we might get a salary and benefits in exchange for our commitment to do our jobs. At home, it might be to carry out domestic duties in order to create a clean, tidy and orderly home (or to keep other people at home happy about our contribution). At college, we commit to our studies as part of the process of learning and achieving the academic qualification we seek.

The key point is that it is unlikely that we will have complete control over these demands, as many will be pushed on us by others or external circumstances. The secret is how we manage or influence our workload, so it works for us and not against us.

There will be times when workload gets just too much—deadlines, targets, competing demands, pressure from others can all conspire against us. If we feel overloaded, we may feel unable to cope with the pressures, which can lead to feelings of stress and overwhelmedness.

We might think that it would feel great to have no pressures, deadlines or demands but the opposite can occur. If there's nothing, or not much to get up for, nothing to inspire and challenge us, we could get bored, apathetic and demotivated. This can lead to feelings of stress too, albeit a different type of stress.

Getting a workload right takes planning, managing and a bit of luck. But it is possible.

Top Tips

Overwork

Workload audit
Construct a realistic assessment of all the different demands on your time. It might present a daunting reality, but once you have an overview mapped out, it can help clarify what is really important, allowing you to plan and prioritise.

Plan and prioritise
If we feel swamped by work demands, it's often because we don't have a clear plan of how to meet these demands and they float around in a whirlwind of anxiety and stress. Work out exactly what your demands are, how you will meet them and when.

Schedule demands

It is fine to have a plan, but we need to turn this into action for this to mean anything. Action comes from scheduling so we can see a clear timeline and commitment regarding what and when we carry out the action. Schedule difficult tasks when you have the energy, but also identify 'quick-wins' to boost your self-confidence.

Communicate and talk

We can feel the weight of demands on our shoulders and often we might internalise it, accepting this as our lot. But sometimes talking about how this is affecting us can offer positive dividends. Maybe it's a boss who should know we feel overworked and overstressed or others in our family or college tutors. Explaining the impact on us to others can open the door to sharing the pressures or changing the workload demands.

Perfectionism doesn't exist

There's nothing wrong with wanting to do a job well but if we believe we need to do so perfectly, we can derive an impossible expectation. We need to challenge the view that just working harder and harder can achieve perfection; a self-imposed perfectionism can lead to excessive pressure on ourselves, which in turn is never satisfied and simply perpetuates an unrealistic view of ourselves. Learn to accept that 'doing your best' is much more achievable (and likely) than being perfect.

Delegate to others

We can be our own worst enemy sometimes, taking on tasks that we simply don't need to. Be ruthless and pragmatic.... Are you really the only one who can do the task or who else can help you share the load? Delegation requires trust and faith in others. Challenge the belief that only you can do the task (see the TOP TIP above—you are not perfect!).

Just say no

It can feel liberating to say 'NO' to someone overloading us. It's empowering and gives a sense of control and enhanced self-worth. If you can't say 'NO', work out what is inhibiting or stopping this? Will you lose your job, explode or die if you say 'NO'? Probably not.

Duty of care

All organisations have a 'duty of care' towards their staff and we have a 'duty of care' towards ourselves too. Employers have a responsibility for limiting or mitigating undue pressure and stress on staff. Acquaint yourself with appropriate organisational policies on issues surrounding stress and well-being and, where helpful, do speak to your boss, occupational health or human resources.

Embrace choices

Sometimes feelings of overload emerge because we feel locked, trapped and unable to make any choices. But there are often choices or options hidden beneath the surface. Taking a step back to see the bigger picture can open up wider possibilities. Or consider how someone else might handle a situation, what advice might they give you? Or what would you suggest to them?

Bring in control

If you feel you have some sort of control over what you're doing, you'll feel you're making progress. Even planning, prioritising and scheduling will offer a degree of control as you're determining the what, the how and the when. You're in charge again. You're in control.

Stress and burnout

Despite the best of intentions, you might feel totally stressed and close to burn-out. It's important not to ignore these signs and to act appropriately when you spot them. Are you becoming more irritable, are your normal habits changing in relation to exercise, diet and sleep? What steps can you take to back away, regroup, recover and rebuild?

Under-Work

Boredom threat

If you consider your job to be boring assess why you are bored. Is it what you do, when you do it, why you do it or how you do it? Is it the job or the task, or are other external or family issues conspiring with your boredom? Are you overqualified for your job or in a role which is not making use of your skills? If you can clearly identify what is behind the boredom you are more likely to be able to do something about it.

Lack of tasks

You might need to add extra tasks to your role if you feel underutilised or offer to pick up extra responsibilities. Most organisations are only too pleased to respond positively to this. If this is not possible find ways to occupy yourself that fit your role. If your job genuinely limits your capabilities, seek out any deficiency or fill the gaps at weekends or in the evenings or during your commute.

Managing monotony

If your job has a routineness to it, build in new elements, mini-challenges or extra functions to the role. If you have a creative side that feels underused, think how you can add a new layer of creativity or flair. Just because others haven't or don't do this, doesn't mean you can't.

Under-acknowledged

Enthusiasm, capability and ambition are often highly prized assets. Do the people who make decisions about you appreciate what you can do or offer? How can you make yourself more visible, or what conversations do you need to have and with whom?

Outside life

Beyond work, academic studies or domestic demands, how can you seek out the emotional, satisfaction or achievement nourishment that you require? What hobby or interest could you start or reconnect with? How can you offer your time for volunteering or helping out locally? Who could benefit from your skills and how might you offer them?

Final Top Tips

Get me out of here

If you are perpetually overloaded or underloaded in your job, maybe it's time to leave. What networking, contacts or leads can you muster in advance, or where would you find the jobs which are appropriate for your skills and experience?

Health barometer

Nothing is worth undermining your health, your relationships or your family. Keep an eye on your diet, exercise and sleep. If you notice you are eating or drinking more or less, or needing more or less sleep, these may be warning signs that you need to make changes.

It's good to talk

Sometimes talking to a boss, tutor, family member, therapist or coach can defuse your stresses and pressures in a way that offers a potential way forward, or it gives you a chance to ventilate your tensions. Keep to the positive though, and avoid any self-defeating and spiralling negative talk.

Action Plan 1: How to Work SMARTER

Workloads are more manageable when your tasks are SMARTER.

Specific	clarify exactly what is required
Measureable	where will you start and when will you know you have finished?
Achievable	ensure your task is achievable and appropriate
Resourced	get the tools and skills you need to complete the task
Timely	schedule the time required realistically
Engaged	connect with others and seek their involvement (delegating) or help
Rewarded	acknowledge your achievement when completed—pat yourself on the back!

Adapted from Doran (1981).

2

Choice and Control

Spotlight

How much control do we really have over our life or our work? Many consider that they are on a conveyor belt of life, destined for a path that our circumstances determine or others dictate. This can be comforting and reassuring for some who crave structure and order. But it can be stifling and limiting to others. We need to find our own acceptable level of choice and control.

When we talk about being 'out of control' we often mean we don't have structure or order and that chaos swamps us. Chaos is disorder and disorganisation. But bring in order and organisation and you create structure and reduce the turmoil. There is a degree of predictability in the unpredictability of life; we can't control the weather or the changing seasons just as we can't choose not to get older and age. Some things we just can't control or change.

But there are things we can control (or choose)—we can choose to wear wet-weather gear when it rains, we can change our activity and exercise routines based on our changing physical capabilities. And this introduces choice. We can choose to wear shorts and T-shirts in the rain, or we could trek across the Antarctic at the age of 80. Neither of these are very sensible or practical (or recommended) but they illustrate the spectrum of choice.

We can feel stressed if we feel we are not in control, but why do we need control? Why is it so important and crucial to our survival? It's not. But choice is. Choice gives us options. Choice allows us to evaluate options and decide on which to take.

We might feel that some choices are incomparable. Say you are sick of your job, stressed, overworked and underpaid. You might think that's it, no choice. But you can choose to stay (work through a plan to find a promotion, recognition, enhanced self-work, achievement etc.), or you can leave (get a new job with different pay and conditions). You have two options already.

Or you could go part-time and take on another part-time job to fill the difference; or you could take a grievance out on your boss or colleague (if there's clear complicity); or you could learn delegation and assertiveness skills, or find new on-the-job skills to improve yourself.

From a point when you felt you had no control and one option, you now have seven choices—OK, some are perhaps more palatable that others, but choices lead to options and sometimes all options need to be considered.

Top Tips

Calm the chaos

In a world of chaos, it can be difficult to simmer things down. But we need a reality check here—what's contributing to the chaos in your life? Are you colluding with it, contributing or feeding it? Identify what the chaos is and this will help to map out what changes or choices emerge. Take a step back… how do things really look?

Choose your choices

With choice comes options. We're often inhibited by what we regard as a good or bad choice. Until we act on any choice, there's no such thing as a good or bad choice. Choose random as well as well-thought through options. A solution can emerge from an unexpected source.

Creativity for choices

Finding choices when they feel somewhat remote can require creativity and dexterity of thinking. Think 'out-of-the-box', random, unstructured and uninhibited. How can you bring your creativity to bear?

Solution focus

If you woke up tomorrow morning and you had the control/solution you sought, what would be different? If it's getting the kids to school on time, maybe the solution is preparation and planning—that is getting up earlier, getting the kids up earlier, having pack-lunches or school clothes prepared the night before, avoiding arguments in the morning/encouraging each other and so on. Find the solution and you can work out the potential pathway to that solution.

Perception is reality

We often strive for more control in our lives but often it's more about the perception of control, rather than the reality of it. We need to believe that we have order and organisation even if, in reality, we don't. And that can be enough.

Decisions decisions

Chaos and lack of control are often caused by a lack of decision-making. Taking control can mean making decisions and choosing to act. Seek out sufficient information to make a decision and go for it. Sometimes you just have to make a decision without being sufficiently informed, in which case, trust your intuition.

You control you

You might not be able to control some things, but you can actually control how you think, feel and behave towards events. Embrace and absorb the range of choices that can allow you the freedom to think, feel and behave in a whole host of different ways.

Distraction attraction

If you feel swamped in chaos, do something, anything. This might be listening to music, reading a book, going for a walk. The mere act of distracting yourself has allowed you to choose to do something and as a result you have introduced control again.

Tolerate ambiguity

'I need to know everything'—do you? Probably not. Is it OK to know enough? And what is enough? Sometimes we don't have all the answers, so putting up with a manageable flexibility can be liberating.

OK consequences

Inaction or indecision often comes from a fear of the consequences of making the wrong decision. Find out what you need to make a more informed decision, or trust your gut feeling, or accept that maybe you will have to 'act in the moment' and sometimes you will make mistakes. But sometimes you will also make the right decision.

Acceptance strategy

Once we appreciate that some things can't be controlled, we learn to accept a new, clearer reality. This takes the pressure off things needing to be a certain way. I can't control how long my car will last. I hope it will be a good few years, but I don't know. I'm happy to accept that it will probably last a few more years before things may start to go wrong. That's enough. I accept that.

Leadership

As a parent or manager, you may need to provide some authority, motivation, structure, inspiration and guidance, which can involve making tough decisions. That's your job. Act, learn and act again. Don't be afraid of making mistakes and enjoy learning from them.

Light from darkness

Turn hopelessness into hopefulness. There is usually a silver lining to every tricky situation. For instance, if you're facing redundancy, you can choose to feel redundant as a person, unappreciated, unwanted and unloved ... or you can choose to embrace this as a potential exciting new beginning, the first day of the rest of your life, an opportunity to reinvent yourself, to reappraise your values and needs to try something new, to live the life you've always wanted.

Freedom

We seek control because we consider it will give us clarity and order, structure and certainty. But what if you could shake off the anchors of control and achieve a utopian world of choices and options? How freeing would that be?

Action Plan 2: Choose How to Live Your Life

1. Identify a problem and siphon it through a feeling, thought and action choice filter.

My problem is: _____

What I choose to feel about it is: _____

What I choose to think about it is: _____

What I choose to do about it is: _____

2. Identify your problem and come up with five creative resolutions or choices which could emerge.

My problem is: _____

Resolution Option 1: _____

Resolution Option 2: _____

Resolution Option 3: _____

Resolution Option 4: _____

Resolution Option 5: _____

3. Identify what you cannot control and how to accept it.

I cannot control: _____

…so I choose to accept: _____

4. Why do you need control?

_____

_____

5. Is this real and accurate?

_____

_____

6. What freedom might you achieve if you relinquish control?

_____

_____

7. Project the need for control on to something which you actually can control—a hobby, interest, sport, activity, creative pursuit, entertainment, fun and so on?

I can project positive control on: _____

_____

3

Task Prioritisation

Spotlight

Targets and deadlines—you either love them or hate them. Most people hate them.

Much of our lives will revolve round some set of targets or deadlines. In organisations, we may need to submit a report on time or deliver a presentation on a specific date. During our education, there will be a series of assignments and exams plotted at different times of the year. And at home, we may have a load of family, school and personal demands on our time.

However, targets and deadlines give us structure. They provide a focus. They can give us clarity and order. But all in moderation! It's when we have far too many of them that the problems and difficulties emerge. We can become swamped and overwhelmed, paralysed into inertia, hysteria, frustration, anger or panic (or all five!).

'There isn't enough time, I have too much on my plate, I'm going to fail, my world's going to come crashing down'. Except, it doesn't have to be like this. Yes, sometimes we may need to manage competing demands and juggle a whole range of complex needs (our needs and the needs of others), but there are ways through this.

How we deal with targets and deadlines is often influenced by our past, by our upbringing and even our parents. Our early life experiences can be significant and script our future attitudes and behaviour.

Can you remember taking your exams when you were at school; the cramming of revision into the last few weeks or days and feeling you'd left it all too late?

Or how your parents reacted to deadlines? Did they panic, did they get frustrated or angry, did they take it out on you or did they sail through with a calm and methodical serenity?

How have your friends and work colleagues managed targets and deadlines? Has this experience given you a model of what you might do, or perhaps shown you what not to do?

As we beaver to meet deadlines, we can be stifled by feelings of inadequacy, fearing consequences which may never happen. Do we have an internal critical voice which doubts our ability or saps our self-confidence? Do we feel we are destined to fail so what is the point in starting?

But targets and deadlines are not meant to freak us out or trigger debilitating stress. They are simply there to get things done. They are your friends if you let them in.

Top Tips

Inspiration not perspiration

Targets and deadlines can be a way to inspire or motivate you, to show off your potential and what you can do well. Perspiration suggests that you're struggling against the odds. What do you need to do to sail through this more easily and who can help you?

Feel the flow

Consider when you got so lost in a task that you became totally absorbed and perhaps lost all sense of time. This is called getting into a 'flow' state, when your focus, enthusiasm and connectedness take over any negative vibes.

Task Prioritisation

SMARTER tasks to meet deadlines

See Chap. 1 for the SMARTER acronym to help you meet your deadlines with tasks which are Specific, Measureable, Achievable, Resourced, Timely (and you are) Engaged and Rewarded.

Delegate out

Who can take some of the work or pressure off you? There's usually someone who can; it's often just about trusting them to take up the initiative. Or if you can't delegate tasks, can you delegate someone as your 'person to offload to', or your emotional crux or support?

Here and now

How you have dealt with deadlines in the past is not necessarily a reliable indicator of how you will do so in the future. Stay in the 'here and now' and enjoy the fact that you can still learn new ways of doing things.

Space out

As much as you can, space out your targets and deadlines so they don't all occur at the same time. Some will also be more achievable than others, so it may help to prioritise.

Demands by others

Seek clarity to understand and appreciate the impact that your targets and deadlines have on other people. Some stresses fed down by others are their issues and not yours, yet the tasks get infected by these inappropriate stressors. Are the expectations of others reasonable and appropriate?

Keep in touch

Despite the best intentions, there may be reasons why you might not make a target or deadline. As soon as you know you are likely to miss the requirement, it's usually advisable to explain this to your manager or tutor, in advance. Often it's better to give advance notice of a potential target/deadline failure, rather than getting to the deadline and bombing.

Declutter

Ruthlessly ditch the stuff that's getting in the way. That includes going online to check Facebook, Twitter, LinkedIn, the news, sporting results and so on! But, do give yourself time out now and again. It's about getting the balance and knowing what's part of your 'break' time and what's needless gutter clutter. Social media clogs our brains and saturates our thinking space.

Action Plan 3: The Critical Crucial Conundrum

Prioritisation is the most important part of meeting targets and deadlines. But we often consider that everything is equally critical and equally crucial. Use the four sections below to differentiate what is critical and what is crucial. They are not the same thing; CRITICAL has an urgency to it, CRUCIAL has an importance attached to it.

You want to focus on as many of the tasks which are crucial. The better you can get at timekeeping and scheduling, the better you will become at making tasks less critical. Critical comes from being last minute.

Prioritise and schedule your targets and deadlines in this order;

What is Critical and Crucial? [do this first]

1. _____

2. _____

3. _____

4. _____

5. _____

What is not Critical but Crucial? [do this next]

1. _____
2. _____
3. _____
4. _____
5. _____

What is Critical but Not Crucial? [when do you need to do this? And why the urgency?]

1. _____
2. _____
3. _____
4. _____
5. _____

What is Not Critical and Not Crucial? [do you need to do this at all?]

1. _____
2. _____
3. _____
4. _____
5. _____

4

Constructive Criticism and Managing Rejection

Spotlight

The reason why we bunch together 'constructive criticism' and 'managing rejection' is that we often confuse the two as the same.

In 'constructive criticism' the word 'criticism' often gives us the impression of some autocratic, bullying, finger-pointing accusation, and yet 'constructive' is the word which softens and clarifies the intent and purpose. Put them together and you get guidance, potential insight and learning with a topping of collaboration, improvement and positive change, which, in itself, is void of past sentiment, critical accusations and emotional baggage, which often skews our perception of the meaning. Perception becomes our reality in that how we interpret something creates the meaning to us.

To be receptive to the value and benefits of 'constructive criticism' one needs to understand the meaning of 'rejection', which the Cambridge Dictionary defines as:

- *The act of refusing to accept, use or believe someone or something*
- *A letter, etc. that tells you that you have not been successful in getting a job, a place on a course of study, and so on*
- *The act of not giving someone the love and attention they want and expect*

Here we see a much more fixed, limited or closed-off perspective. It oozes opinion and judgement, whereas 'constructive criticism' offers guidance and collaboration. The third sub-definition of 'rejection', above, offers another interesting insight … *not giving someone the love or attention they want* … which connects with a basic human need to be loved.

Our feelings of rejection often get tangled up with our past relationships and the need for love, attention, to be heard, to be listened to, to be appreciated and to be respected. This can also link in with various attachment issues associated with childhood, youth and, as a result, the rest of our lives.

To be rejected for a job is what it is. Our skills and experiences are not sufficient for the role or someone else meets more of the requirements than we do. Our rational minds might accept this, but emotionally, we take this personally. It feels personal because we feel rejected as a person but that is our faulty perception valve kicking in. It is similar for anyone whose job is made redundant. They feel redundant as a person, but it's the job that is redundant, not the person.

We need to be free, willing and able to learn by making mistakes. If we don't ever make mistakes, we will never learn. The greatest learning comes from making the greatest mistakes. But we have to risk, we have to be open to the potential of vulnerability, to take a temporary dent in our confidence. A javelin thrower has to stretch the javelin backwards in order to throw it forward.

Constructive criticism needs to offer motivation, inspiration, clarity, guidance and encouragement. We can probably all nod in agreement to that. The problem often emerges when the person who delivers the constructive criticism does not do so in a way which offers these positive attributes. It might be that their body language gives us a different message, or the timing or location is not appropriate, or it is quite simply HOW they deliver the guidance, which is all wrong. In many situations, it's not WHAT someone says that we hear, but HOW they say it.

Learn to model effective constructive criticism for others and you will start to create a culture around you which works.

Top Tips

Constructive Criticism

Moderate your language

Use words that create a positive context; *support, appreciation, success, ability, collaborative, helpful, improve, positive change, enhancement* and so on, rather than more loaded negative words like *disappointment, disapproval, problem* and so on.

Keep it brief

Only refer to a minimal number of 'learning' points; otherwise a long list will sound like you're bombarding them and they'll either switch off or dig their heels in. Give sufficient time to the meeting in a place which offers adequate privacy.

Offer clarity

Be specific about what you are wanting to say and what you are looking for, giving enough time and resources for any change to be achieved. Check that the person has heard what you are saying and that they understand accurately the context and meaning to the feedback.

Stay professional

It might be tempting to slip into a friendly or chatty mode in an attempt to reassure the other person. However, it is probably better to keep a professional distance which is respectful to the other person and is accurate in the feedback you wish to communicate.

Focus on facts

Avoid opinions or judgements which may be influenced by assumptions, half-truths or inaccurate information. Get the evidence you need to demonstrate the need for any change and allow the person to offer any corrections, explanations or clarifications. If constructive criticism is required because of a behaviour or attitude, explain the effect their behaviour has on others as well as how it doesn't fit your working culture.

Moderate tone, manner and style

If someone knows you are going to be giving them constructive criticism, they may already be feeling anxious and vulnerable, which might make them less able to hear and take on your feedback. Soften your approach, as appropriate, to put the person at ease but without losing the intention of what you need to achieve. Again it's about HOW things are said, which has the greatest impact. Be aware of emotions (yours and theirs) and reflect on or acknowledge whether these are helping or hindering the conversation.

Own your perspective

Contextualise feedback: 'This is something many people have struggled with…' or 'many people find this difficult but work through to a solution …' Also set out where you are coming from: 'this could make a really important contribution to the team' or 'I can see a great chance for you to make a big difference' and so on. Use positive adjectives to create emphasis, that is 'make a BIG difference' versus 'make a difference'. People pick up on these emphasised descriptor adjectives.

Offer sufficient guidance

The whole point of effective constructive criticism is that it needs to offer *a recommended set of instructions … that aims to collaboratively improve … containing helpful and specific suggestions for positive change.* There needs to be substance, guidance, dexterity, clarity and encouragement. You want the recipient to be punching the air with enthusiasm, rather than tip toeing out of the office like a puppy with their tail down who knows they have done something wrong.

Transparency and openness

A good rule is to provide feedback in a way in which you would want to receive it yourself. Being open and honest contributes to mutual trust, honesty, professionalism and integrity.

Options remove stuckness

In the heat of the moment, the recipient may be starved of ideas or options. Help them with some suggestions and you may unlock the door of inspiration.

Rejection

Link to the past

The way we interpret feelings of rejection often can be traced to early relationship and attachment issues. It's not to say necessarily that we are anchored by emotional baggage from the past, but there may be a plausible and understandable trigger reaction we get at times of perceived rejection.

Spread the love

Rejection is usually associated with other people, particularly linked to not getting the love or attention from others. Attention and love can emerge from helping others.

Stay in reality

Having a realistic assessment of our abilities keeps us in the appropriate universe. If I get rejected from Astronaut training, it's not a personal rejection, it's because the gulf that exists between the required abilities and my actual abilities are about as wide as planet Earth.

Don't take it personally

In most cases at work, rejection is not personal but a reality. Ten people go for a job available for one person. Nine won't get the job. Nine might be disappointed. But how many will feel rejected?—It depends on how you deal with rejection.

Spread the load

What about submitting to several competitions, applying for more than one job, asking a few different people out? If you always have 'another' chance or options, it can mitigate rejection, as you balance a rejection with the hope of success elsewhere.

Action Plan 4: Emotional Association for Feedback and Rejection

Emotions form the spinal tapestry which influences how you interpret feedback, criticism and rejection. You can understand your emotional repertoire or vocabulary better by considering associated experiences from your past.

Write down your most memorable experience associated with each emotion.

- Frustration _____
- Motivation _____
- Enthusiasm _____
- Rejection _____
- Achievement _____
- Disappointment _____
- Success _____
- Exclusion _____
- Inspiration _____
- Joy _____
- Love _____
- Discouragement _____
- Isolation _____

- Encouragement _____

- Ignored _____

How much does your past experience influence how you deal with or respond to feedback, criticism and rejection?

5

Maximising Personal Efficiency

Spotlight

How many times have we said 'there are just not enough hours in the day'? The USA and the UK has one of the worst records for working longer hours at work. But do we really have so much more work than our Continental friends or are we locked in to some negative long-hours culture or are we just poor at time management? You choose what fits you.

Most job descriptions highlight the 'required' working hours per week, yet we can feel pressured to 'fit the culture' of long hours and giving-our-all for the company. It's a commitment that can get out of hand. We believe in the organisation so much that we essentially lose part of ourselves to it. It might be our choice or it might not. But a choice for some makes it more conditional for those who choose not to slog it out.

Maybe there are times when we genuinely need to put in the hours for a key piece of work. Perhaps this is integral to advancing our careers. If we're working on exams, sure, we need to spend time dusk to dawn revising or whatever it takes. But it needs to be all in moderation.

Legislation on employment rights does offer some protection. Organisations also have a Duty of Care to look after our health and wellbeing at work, and to provide a conducive and safe working environment. But it's one thing to have a Duty of Care policy and another for the senior management to visibly model that and embed it into the corporate culture. Actions speak louder than words.

A long-hours culture normalises the working of excessive hours—do we really need to get in to work at 7am and leave at 7pm? It's not necessarily the number of hours we work, but the quality of those hours. Presenteeism costs the UK economy twice as much as sickness absence. Presenteeism is about being at or presenting to work but not being very productive, or being seen to work but without doing much work that is 'the lights are on but nobody's home'. What a waste of hours at work—for the individuals and the organisations.

Top Tips

Work smarter, not longer
It's the quality not the quantity of work that counts. How can you improve your focus, output or productivity?

Have a break, have a quick break
Does having regular short breaks help? Does having a walk around the block or fresh air at lunchtime help? Some people swear by a 15-minute post-lunch 'power nap'. Try different methods out so you know what works best for you.

Hocus Focus
How can you limit distractions that take away from your work capacity? Establish norms surrounding any open-door policy. Can you switch off your email and mobile phone for brief periods to allow you to focus without the 'ping' of yet another message?

Nourishment and Fulfilment
Do something that allows you to switch off from work, during breaks or at home. Creative engagement nourishes the brain, whereas TV, tablets and smart phones can saturate or suffocate it. It's also about finding

activities or interests which connect with your belief system or give meaning to your life. This might be in religious terms, developing a sense of purpose or spiritual fulfilment.

Family and relationships

Give your relationships due care and attention and avoid taking those sneaky work emails or mobile calls. Retain a strict curtain round your non-work lives; otherwise you'll never fully relax or detach from work, and you and your relationships could suffer.

Critical and Crucial

Define what's Critical and Crucial, Not Critical but Crucial, Critical but Not Crucial, and Not Critical and Not Crucial. Prioritising what's important with plenty of time will limit tasks becoming urgent. Start with what's Critical and Crucial and don't get sidetracked with non-Critical tasks which can be time wasters.

To do or not to do

It's deceptively simple but highly effective … write out a daily 'To Do' list, which is basically a list with things 'to do'. You might need to review and transfer some of today's tasks onto tomorrow's list, but enjoy the feeling as you cross off or strike through a completed task.

Hurry Sickness

Some people seem to thrive on meeting deadlines with seconds to spare, putting themselves under tremendous pressure. What would it feel like to start early and finish early, building in time for a break, for a bit of fun and enjoyment?

Delegation for the nation

Sometimes it just makes sense to delegate. You're a human being, not a machine. Trusting others to help you out will be repaid by their appreciation of this trust. Sure, you need to trust people to delegate, but they need your trust to prove it.

Rest and recuperation

To give time to work, you need to give time to rest. Model it, practise it, do it.

Death-bed scenario

No one on their death bed ever said 'I wish I had spent longer at work'.

Action Plan 5: Task Time-Tracker

Do you really know how much time you spend on different tasks? Complete the Task Time-Tracker to help you identify where you spend your time. Use this to make changes to your working week so you make better, smarter use of your time. There may be some 'normal' unplanned tasks and meetings as you deal with issues as they arise, but if they sap your scheduling, it may be worth reviewing how these are managed.

Sample Task Time-Tracker

Week commencing 15/02	Mon	Tue	Wed	Thu	Fri	Total	% of all
Planned job tasks	2	2	4	2	1	11	24%
Unplanned job tasks	0.5		3		1	4.5	10%
Planned meeting	1		1	2		4	8%
Unplanned meeting	0.5	3	1	2	1	7.5	17%
People support/management	1	2		1	2	6	13%
Crisis management	1				1	2	4%
Administration	1	1				2	4%
Phone calls/emails	0.5	1		2	2	5.5	12%
Training and development				1	1	2	4%
Lunch/coffee breaks	0.5				0.5		1%
Time off: absence/illness							
Time off: leave/vacation							
Total	**8**	**9**	**9**	**10**	**9**	**45**	

Your Task Time-Tracker

Week commencing _____	Mon	Tue	Wed	Thu	Fri	Total	% of all
Planned job tasks							
Unplanned job tasks							
Planned meetings							
Unplanned meetings							
People support/management							
Crisis management							
Administration							
Phone calls/emails							
Training and development							
Lunch/coffee breaks							
Time off: absence/illness							
Time off: leave/vacation							
Others? _____							
Others? _____							
Total	—	—	—	—	—	—	

6

Dealing with Difficult People

Spotlight

We refer to someone as being 'difficult' because there's some breakdown in the relationship. This is different to Chap. 7 which specifically looks at 'conflict', which is not necessarily related to a breakdown in a relationship.

A relationship with anyone (boss, colleague or customer) needs to build on, and connect with, some mutuality of trust, equality, respect, honesty and empathy. A person can appear 'difficult' often because they are focusing exclusively on their needs, without any apparent appreciation of ours. We might also feel they are being totally unreasonable, objectionable, vindictive, insulting, offensive and obstructive. People do actually lie, cheat and stab others in the back (metaphorically speaking). Trust needs to be earned.

Thankfully though, usually people are difficult because of more rational and logical reasons; they fear change, they feel under some threat, they feel unsure of their ground, they have real worries and anxieties, or they have 'issues' which remain unresolved and are projected on us.

That is not to say inappropriate behaviours should be tolerated or accepted. Not at all. There's a red line on what is and what is not acceptable behaviour, and this is often the starting point for how to deal with difficult people.

A relationship with anyone is a two-way process. Whilst we may form a view which defines someone as 'difficult' there's also our side of the perspective. What are we feeling and how are we reacting or responding? Perhaps we feel ignored, wronged, hurt, intimidated, misunderstood, undermined or even flatly bullied. Are we forming our opinion based on the pure facts of the situation as it is in the here and now, or are we haunted or tainted by some similar situation from the past which traumatised or paralysed us?

In some cases we might feel the other person has some vendetta out on us and this can feel particularly threatening and destabilising. It can feel like they have it in for us and there's no escape.

Top Tips

Do something

Sometimes inaction can paralyse us as we feel impotent to act. But doing something, however small, can give us the confidence that we have some control, choice and engagement in the situation to give us momentum to move forward.

Talk it through

We might feel on our own with the problem, so it can help to talk it through with someone, but it needs to be the right person. Complaining to a colleague might start factions or collusions. A family member might be more detached from a workplace situation, but they might not appreciate the complexities or feel unable to do anything in their unconnected position. Your boss could be the one to speak to, unless they are the problem.

Different perspectives

It can help to appreciate that you and the person may have different perspectives and this might be the cause of the situation. Assess the differences and similarities to determine potential reasons behind the difficulties. Is there something going on in the other person's life (home or work) which could explain some of the difficult behaviours towards you? It's not to necessarily excuse them, but you might find if they're dealing with a bereavement, then their behaviour to you is linked, complicated or triggered by this 'one off' event.

Respect

You may have a totally legitimate reason for your difficulty with the person but you need to maintain respect and professionalism so this doesn't escalate unnecessarily. Treat the other person as you would want to be treated yourself. It might be difficult but it will usually pay off.

Face the threat

In most cases, the preferable first step is to arrange a private meeting with the person you are having problems with. If you keep it too informal, the issue may not be taken seriously enough. Set out enough time and choose a location where you won't get interruptions. Choose whether you want to take a colleague into the meeting with you, and offer the same to the other. Do you keep the purpose of the meeting sufficiently ambiguous to allay any fears or threats, or might it help to give some clarity of purpose?

Own your issues

It can help to introduce your issue by saying how you are feeling or what impact you have had to cope with. This is not pointing the finger at anyone, but simply owning your own response. This then opens up the next stage of the discussion where you can suggest that you believe their behaviour is responsible for your stress, anxiety or whatever you are feeling.

What do you want?

Go into any meeting with a grasp of what you want out of it. Is it about getting an apology, or a shared understanding, a clarity about behaviours and consequences or some required change?

Change the environment

Keeping a potential confrontational situation to the work environment maintains the formality and work-focus of any meeting. In some cases however, it can help to get out of the workplace … maybe to meet up over lunch outside work or go for a walk together. It can change the formality, soften the focus and introduce a more human exchange.

Accept emotions

A face-to-face meeting is always likely to expose a range of emotions for you and the other person. Accepting that this is possible helps to manage the emotionality as it emerges; there may be anger, or tears or frustrations and much more.

Official responsibilities

Whilst your boss has a managing responsibility for you, they may be the cause. In which case Occupational Health or Human Resources usually have a confidential protocol for dealing with such situations. You may want to 'log it' or you may choose to take more formal action.

Red line

What's your red line on what's acceptable? Does your organisation have a policy which helps define this red line, perhaps a Bullying and Harassment Policy?

Mediation

Most organisations can provide mediation, which offers an independent specialist to mediate between you both. They tend to work to a shared understanding and a mutual agreement to a resolution but it is not legally or contractually binding, unless the process makes it so. Mediation can usually be arranged through Human Resources departments.

Grin and bear it?

In some cases, you might find that it is best for you to put on your metaphorical tin hat and let time run its course. Maybe the other person will leave? Maybe the situation will resolve itself? Maybe something will happen which will change the situation? This is not to say you should suffer in silence, but a natural resolution sometimes does emerge. But this can be a tough choice.

Grievance

If all else fails, you have tried the formal and more formal routes and you haven't got anywhere, you may have the option to raise a formal grievance. You can always withdraw this later, but the formal grievance is a clear escalation process that can make or break a situation. Your organisation should have a policy on what to do to go down this route but do keep your evidence factual. A diary of the events and timeline can help give clarity to what has been happening, including the names of any witnesses.

Get support

Whatever course of action you take, or choose not to take, you may be under considerable pressure and stress. Seek out the support available to you from your organisation, family, friends or externally. Difficult work relationships can have a huge effect on your health and wellbeing so it's important that you find the support you need. See if your organisation has an Employee Assistance Programme (EAP); they can often give an external but confidential and knowledgeable perspective.

Action Plan 6: Difficult Person Situational Assessment

Get facts, thoughts, feelings, considerations and perspectives down on paper to help you decide what course of action to take.

Facts—what has happened? Date, time, place and witnesses? Keep a diary of the evidence.

_____

_____

Feelings—how has this made me feel?

_____

_____

Their stuff—provide some accurate rationale about why they do/did what they do/did?

_____

_____

Your stuff—is anything from your past getting in the way of the reality of this situation?

_____

_____

Clarity—distil an accurate assessment, consider getting an external independent perspective.

_____

_____

Reasonable—What can you reasonably be expected to 'accept'?

_____

_____

Unacceptable—What can you reasonably be expected NOT to accept?

_____

_____

Take control—what will you decide to do next, how and when?

_____

7
Managing Conflict at Home and Work

Spotlight

We all have our own views and opinions shaped by our upbringing, people influences and past work and life experiences. These can be political, social, environmental and economic based on how we see the wider world, or closer to home about how we get on with others at work.

It's very natural and normal to disagree with others from time to time. Life would be pretty boring if we all agreed with each other all the time. Having a view which is different to another's also helps us to tease out and clarify our perspective and, perhaps, learn to adapt and adopt a different opinion.

We all have different wants and needs, hopes and dreams, aims and objectives, motivations and aspirations. And yet, we still broadly get on with others, learning to accommodate diversity and perspectives. However, sometimes we seem to stick to a position which might produce conflict with another. It's often because some issue is important to us, something which fires us up, gives us meaning, belief and passion.

We disagree, argue, squabble, fall out, clash, differ and collide. We may believe our way is the right way and their way is wrong. We may want ours to prevail, to be taken on board by the other. And this is often at the heart of the problem; we may want to stamp our perspective without appreciating the impact or consequence on others. Ten per cent of conflict is generally due to having a factual difference of opinion, with 90% due to the wrong tone of voice, that is it's not what we say but how we say it.

Poor people and communication skills and a dictatorial or autocratic style can ignite the touch paper of conflict, especially when others feel they have been ignored, unappreciated, undervalued or not heard. However, sometimes one has to be firm and remain steadfast when something is in the best interest of the situation. Employees might agree to work harder and faster if they appreciate that the alternative might mean insolvency and a loss of their jobs. A child may want to play in the snow in their pyjamas yet a parent will probably insist on warm clothing to protect them from the cold.

Conflict also emerges frequently when change looms into view. Most people resist change and want to stick with what they know, the familiar and the status quo. The reality is that most do adapt to change well and soon embrace an all new and improved way of doing things, but the initial vulnerability to a new unknown can feel threatening, uncomfortable and unwelcome. We grudge it, and that can translate into a conflict of views, opinions and perspectives.

Sadly, bullying and harassment happens both at work and home. It's about the psychological control to manipulate, intimidate, suppress, dominate or persecute another, usually to the bully's personal betterment or benefit. This type of conflict can be more insidious, subtle and subconscious, like the drip, drip of a slowly leaking tap. It can make the victim feel impotent, paralysed and terrified.

Fortunately, most conflict is something we can choose to work with, so it doesn't necessarily sabotage, damage or ruin perfectly good relationships and friendships.

But it does take two to tango.

Top Tips

Understand empathy
Learning to understand others will give you advance appreciation of potential grounds for conflict. What's going on for them, what's important to them, how might they react, what could be their stuck points?

Negotiate concessions
Perhaps there's scope to compromise on a perspective, so both 'sides' feel they have won some symbolic concession and can move forward to an agreed focus. We don't like to lose, but if we feel we have gained something, it makes acceptance easier and more palatable.

Develop perspective
There is usually always more than one way of doing something. Consider your choices and whether one might mitigate or prevent conflict arising in the first place.

Being heard
Conflict often emerges when people feel they have not been heard. Listen attentively. This means they also need a voice or opportunity to communicate the impact on them. Reflecting your understanding of their position can help them to feel heard and you to be clear of theirs. If people continue to repeat the same anxieties, it often means they don't feel the message has got through.

Reasoning and facts
Others will want to know the substance to your perspective. What is your reason or rational for having your view? Explain with clarity what your view is and why you have this view and this will help you to craft understanding and appreciation. They might not agree, but there will be more scope for understanding.

Say well
Spend as much time as you can planning HOW to say your pitch. How you say something creates more impact than what you say. Attend to

your tone and manner, your body language and where and when you speak so as to present yourself as assertive and clear, yet reasonable and considered. Timing can be crucial, give it the time and space you need.

Agree to disagree

Appreciate that there will be times when a compromise is not possible and two different camps will remain. This can be difficult. Having the ability to remain and retain respect and dignity for each other will help to forge a professional way of accepting the differences. Don't take it personally when you have to 'agree to disagree'.

Personality clashes

Inevitably, we will come across people we do not like. We might find something they do, say or believe in grates with or contrasts with our own. You don't need to like everyone in life, but in most cases you do need to get on with them. Find some common ground or keep your distance.

Parent-adult-child

Aim to keep communication at an adult-to-adult level, rather than being a domineering parent lecturing a submissive child. Treat the other as an adult and they'll usually respect the same in you. Avoid game playing as this often backfires.

Play to the end

Sometimes it might be in your interest to lose one battle in order to win the war. Conceding a defeat can help you retrench your position for a longer-term beneficial outcome.

Emotional de-escalation

Some conflict can be heated and 'in-the-moment' due to emotional outbursts. Learn to manage and take responsibility for your emotions, and if you go too far, apologise when the time's right. If someone rants inappropriately to you, get out of the situation and revisit it later to explain the effect this had on you and, if relevant, whether you saw their behaviour as unacceptable.

Work protocols

Workplaces often have policies in place explaining what constitutes unacceptable behaviour. These can offer you a guide and a defence. Similarly 'house rules' can help to maintain order and an agreed mutuality of behaviour norms. Mediation with a professional mediator can often help, but don't leave it to the very last resort. Try it at an early stage especially if the stakes are high; this can save a lot of heartache.

Action Plan 7: EAC Conflict-Management Model

Empathise – Apologise – Compromise (EAC)

In most cases the EAC Conflict-Management Model works to mitigate or manage conflict situations.

1. **Empathise**

Show you understand the other person's perspective in a way they genuinely feel heard. At the same time, you need to ensure they understand your side, including what it is and why. *'It is important to me to understand where you're coming from and at the same time, I need to clarify my perspective…'*

---

2. **Apologise**

Not for your different perspective, but apologise that there is a difference in agreement, that there is some conflict between you. Apologising for the fact that a disagreement exists means that you are regretting things have reached this position. *'I'm sorry that there is a disagreement we are having but I'm keen to find a way to resolve things…'.* However, if you need to apologise for something you have done or said, get this in and make sure you are, and come across as authentic and genuine.

---

3. **Compromise**

Find some ground you can give and identify some you can take, where you both feel you have some equal movement forward. *I'm prepared and willing to concede X if you are happy to match me on this one by doing Y…'*

8

Redundancy and Retirement

Spotlight

Redundancy and retirement are very different situations but the similarities make them worth clubbing together. Both constitute a significant life event, they may be enforced or inevitable, they may be dreaded or keenly anticipated, feared or favoured and they certainly beckon a significant change in circumstances and a different way forward.

A familiar perspective felt by many facing redundancy is that it can feel particularly personal; they feel redundant as a person rather the job being made redundant. Similarly, retirement can throw up fears and anxieties of moving from a familiar structure of work, set of relationships and routine.

How you deal with both will be very personal in that they will be unique to you and your circumstances, but they don't define your past life at work nor who you are as a person.

Most of us don't like change but prefer the familiar, the safe and the known. Understandably, change resonates with the unknown and the unpredictable. If we like order, structure and routine, then change is the antithesis and threatens chaos and disorder. But that is if we choose to fear it as such.

Redundancy or retirement is what it is. In most cases we can't really fight it or turn the clocks back. We are faced with a new reality. We can choose to embrace this with positivity and possibilities or dread and despair.

We might not be able to change the circumstances surrounding redundancy or retirement but we can change how we deal with it and cope with it by taking back control and being in charge of how we feel, how we express ourselves, how we think and how we act or behave.

Top Tips

Career trajectory

You probably remember a job interview when you claimed the new job opportunity 'pulled together all your previous work experiences' or something to that effect. Your new stage in life also brings you this same opportunity. What can the past map out for you in your future?

New identity

Any big change offers us the opportunity to reinvent ourselves, based on the many facets that make up our character and personality. Freed from a stereotypical work-identity, who do you want to be from now onwards? What is your dream? Is it an impossible dream?

Information, information, information

Get all the facts associated with your new situation. If your job was made redundant, clarify why it happened to help you understand the circumstances and eventually get closure. Are there outplacement, training or redeployment options? For retirement, check your financial situation, what changes need to be made or will you need to budget differently?

Mark the transitions

Like any significant life event involving change, it is worth taking stock of what we might consider to be losses associated with the change; a loss of work colleagues, a loss of old routine, a loss of work persona, a loss of being appreciated for what we did etc. The point is not to suppress real feelings associated with loss, but to mark them, to mourn them ... and then to move on.

Share the load

Even if it feels like you are the only one going through what you are, there will be others sharing your journey, your heartaches, challenges and joys. Find others in a similar situation (you'll be surprised how many there are within your circle) and reach out to them; you never know what opportunities might emerge by doing this, even if it is just empathising or 'having a chat'. If you have one, do speak to your partner; they might be struggling with their own associated stuff.

Wood for the trees

A significant life event like this can make us bewildered and throw us off balance psychologically. We can't see the full picture but only a filtered, tunnel perspective. Step back and identify your landscape in front of you; your values and beliefs, your family and friends, your hobbies and interests and all the many life experiences that have contributed to defining you as the person you are today.

Achievements and legacies

Many people hit a life event and ponder over lost opportunities, things they wished they had done, or things they wish they had not. What is my legacy? What will have been my mark on the world? The answer is 'You'. End of. You will have influenced, inspired, motivated and contributed to joy and happiness to more people than you will ever know.

Write your life memoirs!

Even if it's not going to be a best-seller (but it could be!), what about reflecting on some of the life situations and experience you've had? Maybe a series of vignettes, anecdotes, chance meetings, amusing situations, ironic incidents, lessons learned and surprises enjoyed?

Giving back

Whether retiring or moving from a job, do consider volunteering, even as a stopgap. It'll broaden your horizons, give you additional work experience, maintain social connections and contribute to a feel-good factor. Whether it's conservation or community-based, there are loads of options.

Healthy lifestyle

Use this change as a means to kick off a new health and wellbeing life style, through appropriate exercise, diet and sleep. Establish a routine which could be based on your old work routine to help with the transition.

The new you

Sometimes being forced into a new situation can open new doors which you didn't think ever existed. Look laterally, out of the box, left field. Pick someone you admire, famous or otherwise; what would they suggest you do, what would they do? Imagine you are yourself five years in the future—what advice would the five year older person give you?

Mortality

It's an understandably touchy subject, but significant life events do make us think of our own mortality. We can't change the fact we will all die one day. Would putting plans in place offer you a reassurance and give you the end-of-life choices you want and deserve?

Fulfilment and purpose

Most of us rarely dwell on this, but now you have a chance to really scrutinise what gives you meaning and purpose. What drives you, makes you passionate, inspires you, excites you, enthrals you, energises you, motivates you, surprises you and delights you? Find it and live it.

Action Plan 8: Bucket List Post-Retirement or Redundancy

Whether moving on from a job, semi-retiring or retiring, write down 50 things you want to do before you die. Below, start with the Top 10 you can achieve in the next 6–12 months … and go for it!

1. _____
2. _____
3. _____
4. _____
5. _____
6. _____
7. _____
8. _____
9. _____
10. _____

9

Work Satisfaction

Spotlight

We have called this chapter 'Work Satisfaction' rather than 'Job Satisfaction' as many of us do things which we might not regard as a Job, as such, rather the Work which we do. It might involve being salaried or volunteering, being an employee or an employer, looking after dependents and caring, working in business or the third sector, looking after a family and a home, or working freelance from home and so on. We might argue that what we do is more of a vocation or calling. It's still work.

But what gives us the satisfaction to do what we do? If we are remunerated for our efforts to what degree is our satisfaction associated with this? Is it the people we work with or the customers we serve or the people we look after? We'll all have a plethora of motivations that drive us forward and inspire us. It can be difficult to define what satisfies us with the work we do. We just do it and somehow we enjoy it and get on with it. Or we find something within the monotony and routine which sustains us.

Evidence suggests work is good for our mental health as it gives us a purpose and meaning, or it gets us up in the morning, or provides a routine and structure, or the wage, or a sense of achievement, fulfilment, gratification or vindication, or something to strive towards improving.

It might be difficult to define our own sense of work satisfaction, but we certainly know when the work we do does NOT give us sufficient satisfaction. Perhaps we feel stressed or anxious, we believe we have insufficient skills, or we don't get on with someone, or lack the capacity or opportunity to develop, learn and grow or we have insufficient control over what we do, or we have too much responsibility or not enough or feel underpaid or under-resourced.

No work can give us 100% satisfaction; things will always conspire against us. But what is 'enough' for us? It's like those who believe they are perfectionists. There tends to be a negative self-fulfilling prophesy about never reaching the absolute pinnacle of anything as it's impossible to be perfect, so this feeds the spiral of needing to 'be better' next time, building the cement blocks of frustration, stress, intolerance, self-hate and self-criticism.

Satisfaction means contentment and fulfilment, not necessarily 'happy', over-the-moon or ecstatic (though these can emerge too). What if it is good enough to be about 80% or even 70% satisfied by your work? Now that sounds a lot more achievable … and satisfying.

Top Tips

From within

Satisfaction comes from believing you have done a good or a great job. You have applied yourself, you've done so in the time and with the resources you had and now you have a content and maybe even a smug feeling inside. You feel satisfied.

Control it

Frustrations and stress can emerge when we feel we do not have sufficient control over what we do. What can you do to bring in more choice in your work? Or if you can't control your work, can you feel or think differently about it? No one controls your thoughts and emotions but you.

Frustration nation

Frustration is a very important emotion which tells us there is some conflict within us or connected to what we are doing. But what's behind it? Peel back the onion layers and you'll find the root cause or annoyance, irritation or block. How can you shift or change it?

Emotional awareness

Other emotions can also send us crucial signals which, if found and understood, give us the chance to act. Anger, for instance, might mask realities of injustice, incompetence, maltreatment, prejudice, unfairness and inequality. Once we know the substance behind the emotions, we're better able to do something about them.

Work/Life balance

The stuff we define as work needs to be balanced with other parts of our life which are not work, such as hobbies, interests, being with family (or being away from them), being with friends, doing other things that interest, fulfil and nourish us. It doesn't really matter what the 'other bits' are, as long as they provide us with a rest from, and balance with, work.

Achievement and success

How do you define these terms? And how do you celebrate them? Are they achievable and realistic whilst still stretching you and your capabilities?

Stress triggers

We define stress as a feeling of pressure that goes beyond our ability to function or cope. What is a healthy, motivating and challenging pressure to one person may be totally stressful for someone else, and vice versa. What are the sources of stress for you and what can you do to reduce the sources or get the resources to help you manage them better?

Counterproductive chit-chat

If you feel frustrated or annoyed with your work, it's often tempting to complain or bicker to others, on the assumption that this is 'getting it off our chests' or ventilating our tensions. But it could undermine your position, fuelling further resentment and colluding with other negative vibes surrounding you. If you need to speak to someone about your frustrations, do so with someone who can help you resolve or improve it. Try to be clear what can be done to improve and resolve the situation.

Act, don't grumble

If you really are frustrated or unsatisfied at work, do something about it rather than moaning about it. The mere act of feeling you are doing something to improve the situation can have beneficial consequences as you have made a conscious choice to bring more control over your situation.

People power

Don't suffer in silence. Expand your network of contacts, connections and affiliations surrounding you and your work. They may offer you a different perspective or new opportunities. If you are really stuck, think about having a chat with a coach or therapist; they might be able to help you find solutions or a way through your predicament.

Life's too short

In some cases, maybe you need to change your work situation and get out. But beware of the lure of chucking your job in for the benefit of smug satisfaction, which could be short-lived. Act in haste, repent at leisure. But, at the end of the day, it is your choice. And you do have choices.

Action Plan 9: Personal Work Satisfaction Survey

Work through the following short survey of statements, selecting the boxes which apply.

	Disagree	Neither	Agree
I have sufficient control in my work	☐	☐	☐
I feel encouraged and supported	☐	☐	☐
I feel fulfilled in my work	☐	☐	☐
I am free from stress most of the time	☐	☐	☐
My work skills are well matched	☐	☐	☐
I have the resources to do my work	☐	☐	☐
I have a good boss (if appropriate)	☐	☐	☐
My work demands are appropriate for me	☐	☐	☐
I am learning and developing as I work	☐	☐	☐
I feel sufficiently rewarded by my work	☐	☐	☐
I enjoy going in to work most days	☐	☐	☐
I understand what is expected of me at work	☐	☐	☐

Reflect on the choices you selected which correspond with any 'Disagree' or 'Neither' answers and start to choose what you will do about making the necessary changes, talking to the right people and making the adjustments necessary.

_____

_____

_____

_____

_____

_____

_____

10

Effective Delegation

Spotlight

One of the big sources of stress for many of us is workload; having too much to do and not enough time to do it. This might be because the demands on our roles are excessive or we take on more than we should. Sometimes we think we can do anything. In reality we can't do everything. Either way, one of the solutions is to learn to be better at delegating some of this work to others who have the capacity and capability to do so.

It can be difficult to delegate as we often believe only we can do the task properly or to our apparent high standard. But we won't know until we try it. We need to let go and give others a chance. It's about trust on both sides; giving over trust to others as well as allowing others to earn the trust. What if someone could do the task at least as well as you, if not better?

Teamwork is about working as a team, which doesn't happen if you're hoarding the workload and probably stressing out unnecessarily in the process. Working with others provides the opportunity for team cohesion, engagement, inspiration and development. The fact is, the more you delegate, the more you can get done. Many successful entrepreneurs are not superhuman but tend to build an effective team around them who carry forward and deliver their plan. They delegate effectively.

A familiar block to delegation is perfectionism, where we believe things need to be done in exactly the right way. Apart from this being near to impossible for any length of time, it takes away the reality that most things need to be done well, but not necessarily perfectly. There's no room for human error or leverage. And because of this, we don't trust anyone unless we believe they will do the job perfectly. But what about 'good enough' or 'well'?

If we don't think someone will do a good job then it's probably up to us to give them the tools or skills to do so. This means that an integral part of delegation is the need to teach, educate, mentor and coach as well as to ensure the resources are available. If we demonstrate how to do a task we want to delegate, then not only do we reap the benefits of shared workload, but we have helped a colleague to learn something new and develop.

Sometimes we might be control addicts; needing to be in charge of what we do. But if you were hit by a bus tomorrow and no one really knows what you do or how you do it, then you're going to create a massive void. OK, if you really were hit by a bus you might not care about that, but the point is that you're not being a team-player.

Top Tips

Trust others

Most people want to do a good job, not just you. Whilst trust needs to be earned, you have to provide the opportunity first, or it doesn't happen. The more you trust, the more likely it will be returned and rewarded.

Respect others

Aligned to trust is the concept of respecting others to take on your delegated task. They'll respect you more if you respect them by delegating. But this is different to dumping; delegation is much more considered and certainly gives a suitable time frame rather than a panicky deadline which is unachievable.

Choice control

A belief that there's only one way of doing everything feeds the control monster. If you consider and allow choice, you encourage others to find their ways to do the task, which might be better than yours. It's a nice trade-off; if you have concerns about whether someone could do a job as well as you, try delegation and you may find they actually do a better job.

Count the consequences

Sometimes we have irrational fears and anxieties about devastating consequences if we delegate a task which is not completed the way we want it done. If in doubt, check it out.

Mentor and coach

You wouldn't expect to drive a car before learning how to drive. We all need to learn and someone needs to teach us. Effective coaching and mentoring allows us to share our wisdom and pass on our insights. It'll act as a guide to educate before, monitor during and review after the task has been completed.

Communicate, collaborate and demonstrate

Show what it is you are looking for and explain this clearly, giving examples, options or suggestions.

Listen, ask questions and seek clarification

Hear any concerns, anticipate queries and check for potential blocks or inhibitors.

Leadership skills

At the heart of effective leadership is the ability to lead others. You can lead a horse to water but you can't make it drink it. The horse needs to want to drink and know how to drink. You need to encourage, cajole, coax, persuade, inspire and motivate; all leadership skills. But you also need to be specific and clear in any task.

Skills and resources

If others have the tools to do your task, and you have confidence that they do, then it's going to make it easier for you to delegate. Focus on providing the skills and resources required.

SMARTER delegation

To give you structure to delegate, apply the SMARTER principle—ensure your task is Specific, Measureable, Achievable, Resourced,

Timely and provide Engagement and Rewards. This will help to provide structure and facilitate review and assessment.

Give it time

Invest sufficient time, energy and resources in the delegation process, rather than rushing it; otherwise you may set yourself (and the other person) up for failure. Consider this time put in as a short-term investment for a potential long-term gain.

Action Plan 10: Delegator Selector

1. Choose a task you wish to delegate.

_____

_____

2. On the graph below, the x axis refers to TIME AVAILABLE TO DELIVER and the y axis is SKILLS and COMPETENCIES (from low to high).
3. Draw a cross for each team member based on your perception of their time available to deliver and their skills and competencies to deliver it.

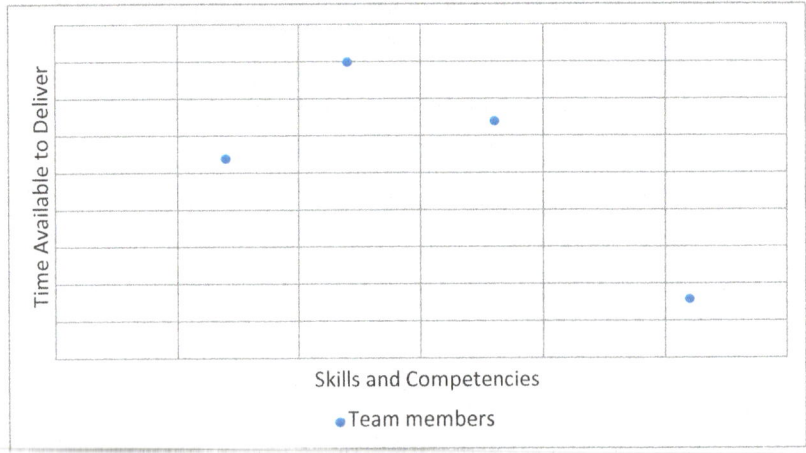

4. Do you select someone with the time to do the job but with lesser skills or delegate to someone you know is more competent but may not have the time? You choose.

_____

_____

11

To Know or Not to Know

Spotlight

On 12 February 2002, in response to a question in a news briefing, the United States Secretary of Defence, Donald Rumsfeld, provided us with a cracking explanation of 'knowing';

There are known knowns. These are things we know that we know. There are known unknowns. That is to say, there are things that we know we don't know. But there are also unknown unknowns. There are things we don't know we don't know

Make sense? Probably not.

Mr Rumsfeld didn't know it at the time but he did rekindle the conversation about what we know and what we don't know. We have an insatiable desire to know stuff, to have an awareness of something through the acquisition of knowledge and information through inquiry or observation.

Our educational systems put a lot of emphasis on the pursuit of knowledge, often at the expense of learning, thinking, feeling, acting and being.

Grades, awards and qualifications bear testament to our knowledge and this sets the life-long quest to know more and more. But we can't know everything.

We can enjoy learning and finding out about things. We acquire knowledge from books, the internet, television, radio, print and online media and through our daily interaction with work colleagues, friends and family. If we knew everything life would be a bit dull—nothing new to learn, nothing to get inquisitive or curious about, question or explore.

And yet we can feel stressed about not knowing enough, whether it's about our work and job or our relationships and social connections. Maybe we feel somehow deficient, neglectful or stupid. Or is it that we don't like to make mistakes and knowledge can prevent this happening? Yet, it is true that knowledge doesn't stop mistakes happening but learning from them and applying that learning does.

The question is not how much we need to know, but what we need to know when we need it. That sounds a bit more manageable and doesn't preoccupy us with all those 'unknown unknowns'.

Top Tips

Structured timeliness

Give yourself a sufficient period of time to gather the facts when you need them, where to look or who to ask. Panic emerges when we need something fast and we can't find it.

Risk making mistakes

We learn from our mistakes and learn the hard way from our bigger mistakes. But this doesn't mean that mistakes are wrong or preventable. They just happen. We can learn to reduce or minimise mistakes, but there will always be some inevitability about the human capacity to make mistakes.

Questioning curiosity

Enjoy the opportunity to be inquisitive and ask questions. One thing often leads to another. Encyclopaedias, text books and the internet provide us with limitless possibilities, thwarted only by time and the direction of travel.

Know or ask?

Sometimes the need to know something is based on the requirement to have a definitive answer but often we can find out more by asking a better question. Be a disruptive thinker rather than a robotic information library. Many new inventions or discoveries occurred by asking a different question.

Vulnerabilities

We can feel unguarded, unprotected and exposed to feelings of self-ridicule if we don't know something we need at the time we need it. But that's normal. It's easy to say 'I didn't know that but I do now'.

Forgetfulness

Barring brain-deteriorating illnesses, we all forget things we have known now and again. That's also normal. And yet we chastise ourselves frequently about not remembering something. It's OK to forget things as it's our consciousness seeking to fathom some depth which it cannot access. If there is a repeated forgetfulness, investigate if there is a psychological block or physical cause.

Ooze creativity

Develop your imagination, inventiveness, ingenuity and originality by the routine exercise of your creative side, however you best express it. The most creative people are ones who think 'out of the box', searching for new angles or perspectives, and doing so they stumble across a new way.

Experience

We acquire knowledge through experience and life events over time, some planned, some unplanned. Think of an adventure you have experienced, maybe as a child, and the unknowns or uncertainties which existed, and yet this probably made this a more memorable experience. Life has risk. Embrace it.

Need to know

Temper the perceived requirement to know everything by considering distilling this into a 'need to know' basis. What is necessary and sufficient?

Known unknowns

Despite the truly amazing advances in medicine, we still don't really understand how the brain fully functions or how to cure some horrendous diseases. This doesn't stop us looking or asking questions but it does normalise our not knowing when the wealth of human existence cannot know certain things.

Ask a friend

Appreciating that you won't always have the answer, there is probably someone you know who does, or they may know someone who does or where to look.

Uncertainty into opportunity

A known unknown opens up the potential for choices and options as we seek out, explore, ask, dwell, consider and find potential answers. Turn an uncertainty into an opportunity.

Action Plan 11: The 'Need to Know' Model

There are certain things we might be expected to know. Conversely, there are many things we are not expected to know. Which is which is determined by the expectation we have of ourselves and our situation, as well as those of others.

For example, as authors of this book, we need to know what we are talking about in order to share our experiences and insights with you. These are our Known Knowns. In some cases we have further researched or consulted with others to satisfy any Known Unknowns. Our Unknown Knowns may include some Top Tips which we don't know but others might. And our Unknown Unknowns are the bits which we would not be aware of, or expected to, include.

Understanding the expectation of what we need to know helps us to act accordingly, to seek out further advice and information or just go with the unknowns.

If you have an issue which you believe you should, or might be expected to, know about, select which quadrant it best fits. This may help you determine whether you really need to know.

KNOWN KNOWNS	KNOWN UNKNOWNS
UNKNOWN KNOWNS	UNKNOWN UNKNOWNS

12

How to Get on in Your Career

Spotlight

Most of us follow a career path mapped out by our earlier education and a combination of variables such as parents' jobs, our personality, location and socio-economic grouping. But the 'job for life' of a generation or so ago rarely exists anymore. Opportunity is now considerable and the availability of training, development and education offers us a choice like never before. Not only will we change jobs several times in our lives, but it's quite likely we will also change careers and where we live.

Whether we consciously plan for our career or settle where we are, or zig-zag from one to another, most of us have some choice over what we do. But we're usually too busy doing our job to reflect on where we are, where we want to be and how or when we'll get there. Promotion opportunities may emerge, or they may not and we change jobs. Often though, it's about creating your own opportunities and you can do that by taking stock of where you are today and what you are doing.

Experience counts for a huge amount and can trump education. Qualifications may get us into the interview room, but experience and what we have achieved in life and work will get us the job. Even seemingly innocuous hobbies, sports, activities, interests and pastimes can illuminate a character and personality dexterity which can give us the edge over a fellow interviewee.

We might be very content and comfortable doing what we are doing and feel relaxed about staying put and plodding on, but inevitably things change. Demands may increase; technology, processes and systems improve; qualification requirements expand; competition increases between organisations and within; companies go bust or get taken over; and there's always the next influx of people into the job market. Nothing stands still and we shouldn't either. Even to protect our current position, we may need to be looking over our shoulder to monitor potential threats.

Career planning suggests a whole-of-life strategy, yet it can last as long as it needs to. Change, by choice or circumstance, will probably dictate the longevity of our plan. Career development, however, is a continual process, where we learn, adapt and develop 'on the job'. This in itself might trigger a change which we determine. Sometimes we hit a ceiling where we become bored or stagnant in our jobs, or we might just hate the work we do or the people we work with. Continual career development will undoubtedly help give us more options for change when we need them.

Top Tips

Networking
It's often said that it is who you know rather than what you know which helps you in your career. Meet as many people as you can and ask loads of questions. People like to help and your inquisitiveness may open up new opportunities with the right people.

Find a mentor
A mentor is someone in your industry, profession or organisation who is more experienced and senior, and able to impart their wisdom, influence and insight to guide and develop you through your role and beyond.

Values and beliefs
What is important to you and what matters most? What motivates, inspires, excites, captivates, enthrals and gives you purpose and meaning? And where can you find this?

Who are you?

Even if you have a pretty good idea who you are, there are many personality tests available online which can give you an insight into how you tick. These can also indicate the types of job, function and team roles more suited to you.

Create a plan

Whether it's developing in your current role or moving on, start by creating a plan for yourself over the short, medium and long term. This will give you a stage-by-stage stepping stone to options. Find a career advisor, career psychologist or coach to give you professional insight, guidance and advice.

Update your resume/CV

Keep your CV up to date, adding in recent achievements and successes. Often looking at what you have experienced to date can inspire you to make the next move that suits you.

Skill up

What can you do to make yourself more attractive to your current or future employer in terms of skills development? Is it a vocational training, updating of skills, continual professional development, a college or online course or something which is readily available through your work?

Job audit

Spend time to reflect on your current role, what you like or dislike and how you can get more of the former and less of the latter? We can be quick to jump ship when the best options may be actually to remain with our current employer. If you feel stuck in a rut, what can you do today to change this with your employer?

Advice

Imagine you were on your death bed looking back at your life; what advice would you give to yourself now? Or pick someone you admire or respect; it might be a historical figure, a sporting legend, celebrity or influential leader—what advice would they give to you about your career?

You are the block

Are you holding yourself back from greater potential? Do you need to brush up on skills, or make improvements, or increase your self-confidence or self-worth?

Hobbies and Interests

Keep up and nurture all the things you do when you don't work. Sometimes you may get the opportunity to turn an activity you pursue for leisure into the job you always wanted to do.

Enjoy now

Whilst you keep ahead of the game and ahead of the pack, don't lose sight of what you enjoy in the here and now. Your current job may just be the best job out there for you.

Action Plan 12: Personal SWOT Analysis

Write down all the Strengths, Weaknesses, Opportunities and Threats which you can identify as they apply to you today and this will give you some pointers to actions to take so you can increase and enhance the Strengths and Opportunities and reduce or limit the Weaknesses and Threats.

What are your STRENGTHS (skills, abilities, achievements, successes etc.)?

1. _____

2. _____

3. _____

4. _____

5. _____

What are your WEAKNESSES (deficiencies, skills shortages, work limitations etc.)?

1. _____
2. _____
3. _____
4. _____
5. _____

Where are the OPPORTUNITIES (internal/external, networking, contacts etc.)?

1. _____
2. _____
3. _____
4. _____
5. _____

Where are the THREATS (skills, organisational change, job instability, competition etc.)?

1. _____
2. _____
3. _____

4. _____

5. _____

The origins of the SWOT Analysis remain unclear though some have attributed the model to Albert Humphrey of the Stanford Research Institute in the 1960s and 1970s.

13

Confident Public Speaking

Spotlight

Few situations generate as much anxiety and stress as speaking in public. Sure, you get the seasoned motivational speakers leaping across the floor bouncing off flip charts, or comedians basking in the raucous laughter of the tear-faced audience, or politicians heckling each other randomly like a tea party of jackdaws, but they sign up to all that. The majority of the rest of us don't routinely speak in public, so when we do, it's an issue … a big issue.

There is always the worry that our voice wavers, or we start to blush, or we forget a key point, or end up mumbling incoherently, or that beads of sweat emerge on our forehead or we get that annoying eye twitch which we think everyone can see, or that the audience thinks we're stupid, or the audience falls asleep, or that the audience thinks we're stupid and then falls asleep. It's the stuff of nightmares which is also guaranteed to keep us awake the night before, rendering us a bleary-eyed, blotchy-faced, emotionally exhausted wreck even before we even get up there.

At least that's probably the worst case scenario. Has all that happened to you before? Exactly. It's never that bad yet there's something in public speaking that shovels coals onto the fire of negative thinking which triggers the emotional tsunami of anxiety and panic.

© The Author(s) 2019
R. Hughes et al., *The Wellbeing Workout*,
https://doi.org/10.1007/978-3-319-92552-3_13

At the end of the day all we want to do is do a good enough job, communicate what is intended with sufficient conviction and emphasis, get some positive audience reaction and achieve a number of empathic smiles and nods of agreement along the way. Has all that happened to you before? It probably has to most of us.

The paralysis of public speaking is all within us and we can change that with a hefty dose of positive thinking, a challenge to negative beliefs and practice … and more practice. Our fears and anxieties are often irrational, unfounded and inaccurate. Being in front of a number of people, we may feel exposed and vulnerable and yet waiting on a platform for a train with 500 fellow travellers is not a problem. In both scenarios, you're in a place with lots of normal people like you and me.

Our audience is generally there because they want to be there, they want to hear us, they are interested in us and want to hear what we have to say.

Top Tips

The end

Think how good you will feel after you have completed your talk. Sense the metaphorical massage of relief, release and relaxation stroking over your body and you'll start to feel good already. Keep that feeling, savour it and bring it with you to your talk.

Plan to do well

Clarify who your audience is so you pitch it accurately; explain what you will aim to cover and the context; structure into a beginning, middle and end; nail your points of learning, summarise and reiterate your key points. Know your subject.

Calm breath

If you feel nervous before your talk, take a deep breath in through your nose over four seconds, hold for 4 seconds, then breathe out through your mouth over 4 seconds. Repeat four times. It's probably advisable to do this in private rather than in front of your audience.

Practice, practice, practice

You'll give yourself a bucketful of confidence if you practice giving your talk, either in front of a mirror, or to your partner, friend, dog and so on. Think about the key messages you want to emphasise. Do it until you feel you have mastered it enough or you are sick of hearing your own voice.

Stories and anecdotes

Lighten your talk with vignettes and stories to illustrate what you are talking about. This limits your talking from a script or from a screen. It's much easier to ad lib a story you are familiar with and it makes your talk more engaging.

Music or audio aid

Add some variety by introducing a video or audio clip, or a piece of music which reflects or emphasises something you're saying. It'll give you a breather too.

Interact with your audience

Offer some leading questions: 'has anyone else experienced this too?', 'is this familiar to you?'. Maybe even plan for a colleague to respond which can reinforce a point you are making.

Presentation aids

Lots of text on a screen can distract the audience as they try to read everything and lose your narrative in doing so. Keep text to bullet points and expand on them. You're using them to explain what you're saying not necessarily lecture the audience. Index cards or prompts may help you.

Pace and pause

Keep up a steady pace but not too fast or you may lose your audience. Inject some short pauses for dramatic effect.

Stay firm

Avoid swaying back and forth like a sunflower in the wind. Stand tall, stand firm and by all means walk about, in moderation, stopping when you want to emphasise something. It's not just what you say, but how you say it.

Stage nerves

These are potentially good! Even the greatest theatre performers can become very nervous before going on stage, but they are able to channel this energy in a positive direction.

Perfectionism

Avoid trying to be perfect. No one's perfect. Focus on how you can improve from feedback and experience.

Scan

Your audience will feel connected when you look at them. Scan the room to involve them.

Panic attacks

Nine times out of ten it won't happen, but it's the fear or threat that triggers the uncertainty.

Smile

Feel the positive vibes, embrace this opportunity, go out and give it your best shot, enjoy the experience and smile. It might be your best-ever speech!

Action Plan 13: Confident Public Speaking in Ten Steps

1. **POSITIVITY**—Believe that you will deliver a cracking talk, you're worth listening to and you have something of genuine interest to talk about. Have a picture in your mind how you want to come across to your audience.

   ↓

2. **PRACTICE**—Know what you're going to say, structure it and practice it over and over again. Start with a script, if this helps, and then refer less and less to this. Keep to within your allotted time, allowing a contingency period in case you overrun or for questions.

   ↓

3. **ENTHUSIASM**—Energise yourself beforehand in a way that distracts you from any nerves; listen to some upbeat music from your mobile phone, have a wee dance, punch the air with gusto, and shout out 'Yeehar!' (probably best done in private!).

   ↓

4. **INSPIRATION**—Watch other talks on the internet as this may give you some ideas about how you can present yourself and your material. Even just taking a clutch of cues can give you confidence and assuredness.

   ↓

5. **THE PLACE**—Arrive early and familiarise yourself with your material, where you will position yourself and seating arrangements. Check all your equipment and aids are working, where to access your speech on any computer and if you can call upon any IT support if required; have some water prepared in case you need to pause for a drink.

   ↓

6. **ENGAGE**—Acknowledge early arrivals, welcome them, start up a conversation 'Have you travelled far?', 'Have you had a good conference so far' and so on. This will put you at ease.

   ↓

7. **RELAX**—It's easier to relax if you smile and take long slow breaths so … smile and take long slow breaths as the audience assembles.

   ↓

8. **WELCOME**—Strike up an introductory welcome to your audience 'How are you today, good?'. They might not say anything but you'll probably get a few empathic smiles or nods.

   ↓

9. **STAND TALL**—Position yourself with authority and a command of your audience. You have the floor. You're in charge now. Give it your best shot.

   ↓

10. **GO FOR IT!**—Sure, you might still be a bit nervous, but this is normal. Most seasoned performers have 'stage nerves' which they harness into focusing on what they're ready and prepared to unleash. Go and unleash. Good luck… you'll be great!

14

The Myths of Perfectionism

Spotlight

It has often been an 'in-joke' that an interviewer asks a candidate 'and can you tell me if you have any weaknesses' and the interviewee states 'well, only that I'm a bit of a perfectionist, but I'm working on it'. The point being that the interviewee mistakenly thinks that being a perfectionist is a positive trait. Actually, it has a cost to everyone the perfectionist comes into contact with. It's not a help; it's a hindrance, a dysfunction and an inhibitor.

Perfectionism refers to a set of rigid, self-defeating thoughts and behaviours aimed at reaching excessively high and unrealistic goals. Perfectionism is often mistakenly seen in our society as desirable or even necessary for success. However, perfectionistic attitudes actually interfere with success. The desire to be perfect can both rob you of a sense of personal satisfaction and cause you to fail to achieve as much as others who have more realistic ambitions and objectives.

If you are a perfectionist, it is likely that you learned early in life that other people valued you because of how much you accomplished or achieved. As a result you may have learned to value yourself only on the basis of other people's approval. Therefore, your self-esteem may have come to be based primarily on external standards. This can leave you vulnerable and excessively sensitive to the opinions and criticism of others. In attempting to protect yourself from such criticism, you may decide that being perfect is your only defence.

A number of negative feelings, thoughts and beliefs may be associated with perfectionism, such as fear of failure, fear of making mistakes, fear of disapproval, all-or-nothing thinking, overemphasis or 'shoulds' and believing that others are easily successful.

Perfectionists tend to perceive others as achieving success with a minimum of effort, few errors, little emotional stress and maximum self-confidence. At the same time, perfectionists view their own efforts as unending and forever inadequate—they never achieve the unrealistic goals which they set themselves so the vicious circle continues, leading to self-critical and self-blaming behaviour, which results in lower self-esteem, and may trigger anxiety and depression.

Because of this vicious cycle perfectionists often have difficulty being close to people and therefore have less than satisfactory interpersonal relationships.

Healthy striving towards a goal is quite different to the self-defeating process of perfectionism.

Healthy strivers tend to set goals based on their own needs and requirements rather than primarily in response to external expectations. Their goals are usually just one step beyond what they have already accomplished. Their goals are realistic, internal, and potentially attainable. Healthy strivers take pleasure in the process or journey of pursuing the task rather than focusing only on the end result.

Top Tips

Reality check

Being 'perfect' is undesirable, impossible, counterproductive, selfish, self-defeating and an illusion. If you consider this untrue, prove it to be untrue.

You at the heart

Keep your goals, ambitions and objectives focused on YOUR needs and desires, rather than that of other people. Do things for you.

Evidence of success

Whenever you feel the need to be perfect, consider three times in the last week or month when you managed to achieve admirable or sufficient success without you needing to be perfect. This will enable you to achieve things realistically and lead to a greater sense of self-esteem, self-confidence and self-worth.

Opportunity rocks

It's impossible to be open and receptive to change, options and opportunities if you have a fixed structure in place. By maintaining a dexterity towards ambiguity, you open up possibilities which, by their very nature, do not have a clear end point.

Time after time

Set subsequent goals in a sequential manner. As you reach a goal, set your next goal one level beyond your present level of accomplishment. This provides a clarity and ease of pace over the stepping stones of your journey.

Test yourself

Experiment with your standards for success. Choose any activity and instead of aiming for 100%, try for 90%, 80% or even 60% success. This will help you to realise that the world does not end when you are not perfect.

Enjoy the ride

Focus on the process of doing an activity not just for the end result. Evaluate your success in terms of what you accomplished and how much you enjoyed the task. Recognise that there can be value in the process of pursuing a goal.

Emotional barometer

Use any feelings of anxiety, frustration or stress as opportunities to ask yourself whether you have set up impossible expectations for yourself in a particular situation. What do your emotions say about what's going on for you?

Fear check

Confront the fears that may lurk behind your perfectionism by asking yourself what you are afraid of or what might be the worst that can really happen? If you find an answer, ask yourself 'so what?'

Embrace mistakes

Many positive things can only be learned by making mistakes. Think of a recent mistake you have made and assess all the things you can learn, or have learned, from it.

Avoid all-or-nothing thinking

Discriminate the tasks you want to give high priority to against those tasks that are less important to you.

Action Plan 14: Perfection Reflection

1. Consider a recent event with which you would normally seek perfection.

_____

_____

2. Reflect on the tension, pressure and emotions you felt.

_____

_____

3. To what degree did you relax and go with the flow?

_____

_____

4. Was it 'perfect' and did that matter?

_____

_____

5. What was the consequence of not being perfect?

_____

_____

6. How does this change your view, opinion or perception of Perfectionism?

_____

_____

Example

1. I was presenting a report to my managers last Monday.
2. I was anxious, shaking and tense.
3. I couldn't relax and read much from my notes.
4. It felt robotic and didn't seem natural, so came across mechanically.
5. No consequence.
6. I don't need to be perfect. I need to calm myself beforehand, smile and act more naturally.

15

Managing Change in Organisations

Spotlight

Many of us don't like change. We prefer what we are used to; the familiar, the norm, the status quo. With this we have a pattern, routine and structure. It's comfortable. We know what to do, when to do it and how to do it. It provides a protective cocoon within which we have assuredness, certainty and security.

Faced with change, we fear the unknown; we expose ourselves to risk and vulnerabilities, of being less certain of the future, emerging from our comfort zone. A loss emerges; a loss of the stability and structure of before. And a loss can be painful. But nothing stays still for long. The merry-go-round of change means that the only certainty is change itself.

We respond with the normal emotional reaction to treat; anxiety, fear, tension, mistrust, angst, nervousness, panic, concern and doubt. It might also trigger feelings of resentment, anger and frustration. But these are all normal responses. Knowing this helps us to understand and appreciate why we feel or respond the way we do. And how others will too.

Our emotional responses may be associated with real or perceived threats; whether we might lose our jobs, or change our authority, roles and relationships and all the consequences that emerge from these changes.

Sometimes it is the fear of the consequences which can be worse than the change itself. And this is often because we just don't know what's happening or going to happen. It's normal to feel unsure about uncertainty.

Organisations continually evolve to keep up with or ahead of the competition, to respond to increasing or changing demand, to embrace new and better ways of doing things and to adapt to a host of social, economic, cultural and political influences. There's often a domino effect, where one change triggers some sequence or inevitable consequences which organisations need to respond to.

Change is about forging a new way, so there is some unavoidable and undeniable unknown associated with this. It's about building the foundations of the new rather than fighting against the old traditional way. With all foundations, we get the chance to construct a solid platform on which everything else grows and flourishes.

Collaboration, consultation and communication are the hallmarks of effective change management, so we bring together others to explain the need for change, to facilitate feedback and exploration as to how change might emerge, and provide a consistent dialogue so all involved are aware of what's happening.

This ensures that people feel involved and part of the shift, rather than ignored and neglected. It also enables people to understand the impact on them and allow for the dust to settle.

Top Tips

Start early

As soon as the need for change emerges, prepare and plan. Know what needs to happen and ways in which this can be achieved at minimal disruption or unsettlement for others.

Dialogue

When a plan has been put in place, start communication as soon as possible, which will provide some structure and stability to those who fear the unknown.

Involvement

Determine how much you involve others as you evolve the plan. Some will welcome collaboration, but others may experience uncertainty when they need assurance and clarity. We can get a shock if something big happens unexpectedly, so a drip-feed approach may suit most.

Groups and forums

Allow for meetings, forums, consultation groups and representations so people feel heard and make sure there is substance and structure to these meetings, where concerns raised are addressed and responded to. It should also offer an opportunity to influence aspects of the changes too.

Office grapevine

Be alert to the fact that groups of people are likely to chatter and talk about what's going on, and they may ventilate their fears and anxieties which may damage morale, feed negativity and create a subculture of antagonism. Offer an outlet where concerns are raised in a managed and supported environment. Empathise, appreciate and understand what their fears and anxieties are. Contain any in-fighting, gossip or office politics.

Information and expectations

Effective communication of change is facilitated as much by WHAT the change is, as it is by HOW the change is going to happen and HOW it is communicated, discussed, developed and implemented. 'How will the change affect me?' is a more likely question than 'What is the change?'. If people understand the extent or limits on how the change will affect them, they will better adapt to what they need to do. If they know what will be expected of them, they can start to prepare and get used to what will be expected of them.

Decisive not divisive

Focus on achieving clarity through firm decision-making, rather than giving too many options which may otherwise cause confusion, uncertainty and ambiguity. You can't please all of the people all of the time, so some may remain sceptical and suspicious or ... downright hostile and reactive.

Champions of change

Providing as much rationale, substance and information behind the need for change will help others to appreciate and understanding the necessity and increase the chances that the majority will back and support it. Ideally, we're looking for the majority to be ambassadors and champions of the change, so the energy and enthusiasm take over from the fears and anxieties.

Opportunities

Whilst reactions to shifting from the safe and the norm might cause anxiety, harness this energy into positivity and enthusiasm. If people find a real and genuine opportunity to do things better or differently which allows them to do a better job, or more easily, they'll likely jump on board.

Action Plan 15: Model for Implementing Effective Change

Managing effective change requires planned communication, participation and collaboration.

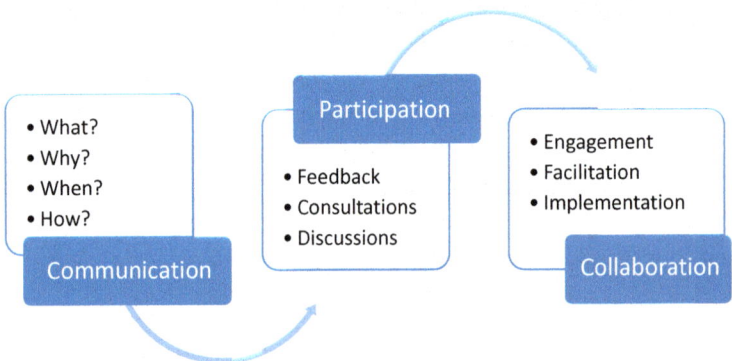

Use this model for implementing effective change to populate your change strategy.

16

Working with Global Uncertainty

Spotlight

Change occurs in organisations because of the need to adapt, evolve and improve in the face of a plethora of variables, threats and circumstances, both internal and external. But there is a wider landscape out there which impacts us all. This is the social, cultural, economic, technological, environmental, spiritual, political and global environment of which we are all a part. It doesn't matter what job we do, the profession we work in, or the size of our organisation, we are all at the mercy of this 'big picture' out there and the world events that shape our destiny.

However much we try to insulate ourselves from, prepare for and insure against crisis situations and world events, we can never be totally prepared for the unexpected, although we can learn to be adaptive, responsive and resilient to these situations. Whether it be the need to stay financially solvent, or responding to advances in technology and changes in consumer behaviour, change is upon us whether we like it or not.

Governments come and go, shifting along the continuum of left, centre and right of politics with as many policy changes as fits their mandate and manifesto. And sometimes it is the people who rise up and make their voices heard and governments respond, or not. Technological, engineering and medical advances offer a new way forward.

Countries jostle on the world stage to exert their presence and prowess; they can focus on self-interest nationalism at the expense of the wider global cooperation and harmony; the environment can be savaged, plundered and destroyed; pollution and global warming threatens thousands of species which will irrevocably threaten the food chain; ethnic cleansing continues explicitly and insidiously; wars are threatened and fought, territories are won and lost; and mass migration in the face of global hostility, social inequality and economic hardship threatens global stability.

And if this isn't enough, the weather chips in with floods, fires, hurricanes and earthquakes; terrorism seeks to force change through fear, intimidation and bloodshed and then there are the more frequent 'smaller' (but equally tragic) traumatic events including road traffic accidents, industrial accidents, suicides, accidents at home, fatalities and serious illnesses or injury.

Whilst much of the above may seem safely distant from our everyday lives, it continues to reap widespread repercussions and consequences in all our lives. The fact that much seems to be sufficiently distant might stifle the inclination to act. However, since the dawn of civilisation, people have been able to come together, grow together, find a voice together and act together in a way that forces change. And social media has an increasingly powerful part to play in forming opinion, attitudes and belief.

Top Tips

Keep calm
In a world of chaos and catastrophe, it's easy to become disillusioned and depressed by it all, but this book is about resilience and humans have a remarkable capacity to stay valiant in the face of adversity.

Positive perspective
Adopting a positive way of being allows us to seek out and search for the good and the great and to find meaning and purpose to the endless good things and happy times we will experience.

Mindfulness

Often, we get distracted by the big picture rather than appreciating the little pictures all around us. Appreciate and enjoy the here and now, the joys, the laughter, the excitements, the successes, the achievements, the happy times and the good times. Life is good all around us if we let it in. Test this out by taking a mindful walk; look around at the colours, feel the breeze on your skin, notice the contours of the land and the shapes of the clouds, listen to the sound of the birds and the rustling grass. Appreciate every breath you take.

Personal responsibility

If something troubles or irks you, do something. Inaction traps and locks us in a pit of apathy. If you feel strongly about something, what action can you take or what choices can you make?

Transparency

Be open about how big issues affect, concern or worry you. It's likely to mobilise an empathic response from others and you'll build a groundswell of camaraderie, engagement and collaboration.

Improvement

Tough times happen, but things usually get better over time. People take action, good things happen. Believe that things will change for the better, or do something to make things better. Even during a tough time you can unexpectedly meet amazing people, such as meeting a wonderfully inspiring family who are supporting a loved one with cancer.

Stepping stones

Focus on what you can do rather than what you can't do. Consider the change or impact you can make, one step at a time. Things don't change overnight but you could be the catalyst for change.

Acceptance strategy

You don't need to agree with the things which upset you, but you can accept that tough and bad things happen and you might not be able to change, influence or prevent them.

Transformational growth

Seek out the opportunities which emerge from the obstacles. Find how you can grow and develop from a personal and professional perspective.

Where's the meaning?

Consider how events impact on your beliefs, values and sense of purpose. What is important to you and why? What can you do to make a difference?

Tolerate ambiguity

Be adaptable to events, so you can sail the choppy waters and navigate through the storms of life.

Contingency plans

What can you do to prepare for events beyond your immediate horizon? What has experience taught you? Trust your instincts and the lessons learnt. Plan for a better present and future.

Action Plan 16: Dealing with Uncertainty which Worries You

Being anxious and worrying about uncertainty can paralyse you into negative-thinking patterns, physical inertia and emotional stagnation.

You become more mobile, adaptable and responsive to uncertainty by taking positive action.

If you can do something about it, focus on this and take action.

1. **What uncertainty are you anxious about?**

_____

_____

_____

2. **Can you do anything about it?**

YES, I can ... _____

_____

OK, so now you can do something about it, take this action and you don't need to worry anymore.

OR

NO, because ... _____

_____

OK, so now you know there's nothing you can do about it, so why worry?

17

Personal Stress Management Toolkit

Spotlight

We experience stress when we perceive that the demands placed upon us exceed our ability to cope. Our perception is our reality. An issue, circumstance or event may not be stressful in itself, but the way we perceive it determines whether we interpret this as stressful.

Stress can also be an accumulation of mini-stresses, which we contain temporarily but potentially don't manage, and then a 'final straw' or 'perfect storm' smashes in and we feel suddenly overwhelmed by the sea of competing demands.

We all cope differently. What is pressure to one person is stress to another and vice versa. Our capacity to cope is influenced by past reactions to stress, life events, our upbringing, how we classify stress as opposed to pressure, our personality, our emotional make-up and our ability to relax.

We all need a certain amount of pressure in our lives to motivate us and get us up in the morning. It gives us targets to reach, ambitions to fulfil and successes to achieve. But too much pressure can tip us into an unhelpful and destructive stress zone, leading to irritability, reduced concentration, lower productivity, skewed thinking and the real risk of making mistakes and having accidents.

It can contribute to depression and anxiety and affect our appetite, sleep and enthusiasm. Therefore, when talking about stress in this chapter we really mean the 'negative stress' or 'destructive stress' which feels very different to pressure. Pressure's fine, pressure's good.

Top Tips

Break it down
Feelings of stress are often an accumulation of mini unresolved pressures. Identify all these impediments and deal with them one at a time.

Identity stressors
We tend not to confront stress until it happens and then it's too late. Preventatively, identify the different issues which tend to contribute to your feelings of stress. Explore strategies to manage each one independently. Write your solutions down so you have them available for those times when you need them.

Stress inoculation
Protect yourself against times of stress by constructing your own 'stress relief arsenal', that is, all the things you can do, think and feel which successfully calm you down, relax you and remove your stress symptoms.

Modify behaviour
What you do contributes to your perception of stress. Review how you might collude with your sources of stress. If you are always late and get stressed by this, then act to ensure you give yourself more time so you are not late.

Moderate thinking
If you are self-critical and self-loathing, you're likely to chastise yourself in a way which creates stress in the first place. Monitor how your thinking contributes to stress. Find ways to deal with negative thoughts through distraction, positive reinforcement or by identifying and

resolving the root causes of your negative thinking. Seeing a therapist or coach can help you find what these might be.

Healthy lifestyle

Eat a balanced diet, hydrate your body, reduce stimulants like caffeine, moderate alcohol consumption, exercise regularly and get sufficient rest. The body and mind are linked and looking after our body is something each of us can do.

Emotional compass

Get to know your emotional repertoire or make-up. Which emotions do you seem to feel at different pressure-laden situations? What are these emotions telling you? Emotions are a massively insightful compass to the direction of your sources of stress.

Action stations

Sometimes we know when we feel stressed but stay rooted and do nothing. Do something, anything and this is often enough to give you a pause for breath, a sufficient distraction, an escape from the situation or a different perspective.

Lessons in stress

We often fall into well-worn stress situations. What have you learnt in the past by way of dealing with stress, or coping better, or reducing the pressure, or changing how you respond to stress? If what you always do doesn't work, try something different. If you do what you always do, you'll get what you always get.

Personal management

If you organise and manage your daily demands with clarity, purpose, structure and order you can really help to plan, prioritise and schedule your working day. Being chaotic, haphazard and muddled leaves you open to a potential hailstorm of stressors.

Get a life

Get some perspective so you are not preoccupied with issues that contribute to stress. Build in an effective work-life balance strategy and seek nourishment from interests outside of work. This includes having a social life or being able to catch up with family and friends, where this helps.

Relax

Most of us are pretty poor at structuring positive relaxation habits—apart from crashing out on the sofa and flicking on the remote control. Learn and then practice relaxation techniques or try guided meditation or progressive muscular relaxation techniques; there are loads of free resources on YouTube or on the internet.

Mindfulness

Become more mindful by consciously becoming increasingly aware of your environment at home or work. Use your senses to absorb, embrace, enjoy and appreciate your surroundings; reacquaint yourself with, and fine tine your, senses of sight, sound, touch, feeling, taste and smell.

Professional support

If you find that you are not coping with stress and can't seem to find what traps you in a vicious spiral of bad behaviours, emotional outbursts or negative-thinking patterns, then try working with a therapist or coach. They can help you understand what's going on for you and will work with you to find the changes you need to make or the solutions you need to find.

Action Plan 17: Stress 'Management Standards'

The UK's Health and Safety Executive (HSE) Management Standards[1] are clusters of conditions regarded as being required to mitigate stress at work. Read through the following list to check that your organisation applies these standards, and if not, consider what action needs to be taken, how, when and by whom.

---

[1] www.hse.gov.uk/stress/standards/index.htm. *Contains public sector information published by the Health and Safety Executive and licensed under the Open Government Licence.*

DEMANDS

- ☐ The organisation provides employees with adequate and achievable demands in relation to the agreed hours of work.
- ☐ People's skills and abilities are matched to the job demands.
- ☐ Jobs are designed to be within the capabilities of employees.
- ☐ Employees' concerns about their work environment are addressed.

CONTROL

- ☐ Where possible, employees have control over their pace of work.
- ☐ Employees are encouraged to use their skills and initiative to do their work.
- ☐ Where possible, employees are encouraged to develop new skills to help them undertake new and challenging pieces of work.
- ☐ The organisation encourages employees to develop their skills.
- ☐ Employees have a say over when breaks can be taken.
- ☐ Employees are consulted over their work patterns.

SUPPORT

- ☐ The organisation has policies and procedures to adequately support employees.
- ☐ Systems are in place to enable and encourage managers to support their staff.
- ☐ Systems are in place to enable and encourage employees to support their colleagues.
- ☐ Employees know what support is available and how and when to access it.
- ☐ Employees know how to access the required resources to do their job.
- ☐ Employees receive regular and constructive feedback.

RELATIONSHIPS

- ☐ The organisation promotes positive behaviours at work to avoid conflict and ensure fairness.

- Employees share information relevant to their work.
- The organisation has agreed policies and procedures to prevent or resolve unacceptable behaviour.
- Systems are in place to enable and encourage managers to deal with unacceptable behaviour.
- Systems are in place to enable and encourage employees to report unacceptable behaviour.

ROLE

- The organisation ensures that, as far as possible, the different requirements it places upon employees are compatible.
- The organisation provides information to enable employees to understand their roles and responsibilities.
- The organisation ensures that, as far as possible, the requirements it places upon employees are clear.
- Systems are in place to enable employees to raise concerns about any uncertainties or conflicts they have in their roles and responsibilities.

CHANGE

- The organisation provides employees with timely information to enable them to understand the reasons for proposed changes.
- The organisation ensures adequate employee consultation on changes and provides opportunities for employees to influence proposals.
- Employees are aware of the probable impact of any changes to their jobs. If necessary, employees are given training to support any changes in their jobs.
- Employees are aware of timetables for changes.
- Employees have access to relevant support during changes.

18

Organisational Savviness

Spotlight

In any workplace environment, there are ways and means of doing things, which can be part of both an explicit and implicit culture. Beyond this, there are also ways in which we interact with others which can help or hinder how we get on, progress and smooth our way through the labyrinth of organisational life.

We all like to work with people we like, who engage with us in an appropriately friendly way, who connect with our vision and ambition and share our pace, manner and style. But we are all different, with complex needs and wants, possibly competing with others internally and externally and forging our friendship and working allegiances along the way.

Being politically astute and shrewd, and having an organisational savviness relates to having the skills to be mindful and aware of how systems, processes and people work with each other, and learning to mediate a path through all this with intuitive empathic awareness. It's like being able to read an unwritten book, spotting the signs and symptoms of threats and opportunities.

At the heart of this savviness is the importance of building effective relationships. You want people to work with you and not against you. Are you aware of things that you say or do which might rile, frustrate or clash with others? You need to understand how you come across to others so a healthy dose of self-awareness is a pre-requisite, followed by empathic awareness, being able to read the signs other people give (or mask) and what they are seeking or wanting to achieve. In other words, 'Emotional Intelligence' (see Chap. 45).

As you build relationships, you also need to build bridges and networks of collaboration. This involves helping others to fulfil their needs and wants so that you can potentially call upon their support when you need the favour returned. Your support needn't be conditional or obligatory, but rather an unspoken, implicit gesture which might be rewarded in the future. In some cases, however, we need to be more explicit so that we can negotiate: 'If I back you with your project, would you support mine?'. Savviness is about knowing when it is better to be implicit or explicit.

Office politics pervade organisations, as people jibber and jabber, hustling in one cluster or another. Be careful about getting dragged into other people's turf battles, dysfunctional group dynamics or whispering gossip clichés. Remember the person who gossips with you has the equal potential to gossip about you! But, and there's always a but, maybe you need to speak to some people to find out what is happening and maybe there is some important substance to the office 'grapevine'.

Being organisationally savvy, shrewd and astute will help you decide how to make the right choices.

Top Tips

Self-awareness

Understand how you present yourself at work. Personality tests may help to give you a steer, or ask others what they think. Do you need to adapt your style or approach to one which 'fits' better?

Watch and listen

Get a sense of what's going on in different situations. Can you identify issues below the surface, non-verbal cues and body language signs? Listen out for the things that are not said.

Need to know basis

Sometimes you may get a sense that something is going on without having access to the full facts. Is there some trusted colleague you can speak to so you can find this out? But, do you need to know? Be wary of contributing to office 'gossip'. Sometimes it is best not to know what's going on especially if it is biased, inaccurate or unhelpful information.

Tact and diplomacy

You might not charge into meetings like a bull in a china shop, but are you sufficiently aware of your abilities to engage with appropriate sensitivity in different situations?

Aim high and negotiate

It can be effective to seek out or ask for something which is more than you need, so you can compromise and negotiate to what you really need. But again, you need to understand how this will be interpreted and whether this could do more harm than good.

Ooze confidence

Believe in yourself so you can project this self-confidence to others to give you a sense of assuredness. However, there's a difference between confidence and arrogance. Create the path that you want to tread.

Who's who

Get to know the thoughts and views, needs and wants, ambitions and goals of the movers and shakers in your workplace. Who has the clout or the influence or access to funds and resources?

Allies and support

Tough times do happen and you may need to call upon or muster some help and support. This is when the time spent nurturing relationships should pay off. Who can you, or need to, call upon? And when is the best time to ask?

Authentic and real

Being real, open and transparent will offer you a clarity about how people see you. But keep something back when you need to, so you don't show your cards too early.

Loyalty and trust

Trust is crucial in all walks of life and needs to be earned. It can be damaged in an instant. Guard against disloyalty. Support your boss and they will (or should) support you.

Big brother

Whilst you fine-tune your political radar, remember others may be keeping an eye on you too. It all works both ways. Project your intensions, honesty, professionalism, integrity, trust, skill and reliability.

Action Plan 18: The 'Who's Who' Model

It's all about relationships. Consider the following questions and write in the applicable names;

Which colleague can you rely on most? _____

Who do you not trust at work? _____

Who can enhance or elevate your career prospects most? _____

Who is most likely to sabotage your career prospects? _____

Who do you need to be wary of? _____

Who has the influence, clout or funds? _____

Who can you give you support in a crisis? _____

Who is a liability and needs to be managed accordingly? _____

Who can most help you meet your work objectives? _____

Who gossips most? _____

Revise this list regularly to help you appreciate the movers and shakers, as well as those to guard against or monitor carefully.

19

Networking and Your Dream Team

Spotlight

Some people find the prospect of networking stressful because it is perceived as something which is manipulative, selfish and exploitative. But that's a misunderstanding of what networking is about. For a start, it's not all about you! Networking is a two-way process concerned with developing quality, genuine and real relationships. It's not about exploiting people, it's about exploiting opportunities. In fact, networking is less about 'how can you help me' and more about 'how can I help you'.

Imagine you see a job advertised and you think 'Ah, that would be ideal for Steve', so you tell Steve about it. He hasn't seen it but agrees, goes for it and gets it. That's an example of an effective networking relationship. You look out for each other and the favour is returned. Incidentally, some 70% of jobs are filled through networking. Whilst you wouldn't specifically expect Steve to need to 'pay you back', you just know that Steve might help you out, or link you in, when an opportunity arises.

It's not all about 'doing favours' but essentially information sharing. We are recipients of information, insight, facts and news and we choose to signpost this to individuals we believe will benefit from it. This knowledge sharing becomes a key facet of networking and the more we share material which is relevant, topical and timely, the more others will reciprocate.

We can gain support, perspective and stress relief by the people we interact with in our home and work networks. In our coaching consultations, we often encourage clients to develop their 'Dream Team'; the network of unique individuals who are key allies, champions and saviours who we can call upon when we need them.

We might have several 'Dream Teams'; maybe one for work or career development, another for family and home life, another for health, fitness and wellbeing, one for stress management and so on. We can alternate from one Dream Team to another, or they might intersect or they might be very specific … maybe have a Dream Team for your home; who do you call on for electrical, plumbing, heating, decoration, roofing, gas work or insurance? It's good to know you have people to call on when you need them. Speak to them all when they are patching up or servicing your home … the benefit of networking is that the benefits spread far and wide and you never know where it ends.

People often take an interest in people who are interested in them, and the same applies to us too. Think of a time when someone showed a real and genuine interest in you or what you were doing? You probably felt quite engaged, connected, listened to, heard, respected, appreciated and so on. But it has to be genuine interest. We can all think of an experience when someone asked us a question and then clearly had no real interest in us or our answer … eyes looking elsewhere or lack of resonance, enthusiasm, interest or connection, or giving incongruent body or non-verbal signals.

Top Tips

Business cards

What's on your business card says a lot about you. What might a cheap DIY faded-print, dog-eared card say about you? Consider having your photo, so people can remember you. Keep the reverse blank or with space to enable the recipient to write down notes, comments or observations.

Elevator pitch

Construct a three-minute 'pitch' about you or the objective of your networking which provides a concise summary, which could interest, and be understood by, a brain surgeon, brick-layer and a banker.

Purpose of networking

Think about what you are trying to achieve with networking. If you don't know, how can anybody else? Is it because you're building up your work profile, or because you're keen to get a new job, or a promotion or work contacts?

Keep to the possible

Don't ask people for the impossible; 'Can I have that job please, thank you?'. But 'Can you give me advice on how to make me a hot prospect for that job?' will be more feasible.

Image and visibility

What is your profile, image or brand? How do others see you or how would they describe you? First impressions might count, but so do the second and third ones. Craft the way you want to be seen.

Active listening

Really hear what people say by reflecting your understanding, showing you have heard them and by asking questions. Learn to hear what is not said or the more unconscious messages which emerge.

Not about you

Resist parallel conversations, that is, when someone says something and you immediately switch focus to talking about your similar situation. People falsely think this offers empathy but it doesn't. It's just an annoying demonstration that you consider you are (or your story is) more important than your conversation companion.

Posture and body language

Be mindful about how you hold yourself. Stand firm and tall, look people in the eye, don't talk too fast, keep focused, be friendly, smile and relax. Be aware what you do with your body, especially folding legs or arms, eye focus, titling of head, scratching and itching and other unconscious cues.

Handshake

Ensure you have a sufficiently firm handshake that you are not so limp that it feels like it belongs to a puppet but also not too hard that you're going to break bones.

Small talk

A lot of people hate small talk, but it's simply a quick 'way in'. Think of topics in advance, the weather, something in the news or an observation about surroundings. Be resilient in pushing yourself forward; if it doesn't work with one person, move on and try with the next—ultimately it's a numbers game. Don't be defined or limited by the one unsuccessful interaction.

Authenticity and focus

Be honest, trustworthy, reliable, credible and approachable. Falseness is often easy to spot. If you feel nervous, that's fine, say so. If you model the skills, behaviours and competencies of the people you are seeking, you will get them. Reach the right people—if you are networking to find sales for your business, go somewhere where people buy what your business sells.

Size does not matter

Those who brag about having thousands of contacts are unlikely to have quality relationships.

Action Plan 19: Dream Team Networking Map

1. Focus on a particular networking focus or purpose, for example, health and fitness.

2. Select the widest scope of Dream Team participants, for example, your doctor, optometrist, dentist, physiotherapist, chiropractor, gym instructor, dietician, pharmacist, coach, Aunt Mable, golfing pal Bob, hiking friends Bill and Ben, badminton partner Sally, tennis friend Mally, soccer friend Hally, fishing colleague Gary and so on.

_____

_____

_____

_____

3. Now consider deleting any from your network who either are too 'one-sided' and focused on themselves or do not meet your core networking purpose. For instance you might consider ditching golfing pal Bob as you usually have too many beers in the clubhouse after a round of golf, thereby defeating the object of health and fitness.

_____

_____

_____

_____

4. Schedule a time in your diary to meet each individual as frequently as is appropriate. Get to know them. And have fun doing this.

_____

_____

_____

_____

20

Spotting Signs of Stress in Others

Spotlight

While this chapter focuses on identifying when others are stressed, it can be applied to you too. The point is that most us don't always pick up the cues when we feel overloaded, so sometimes it can help to get a gentle nudge from someone else.

It is worth highlighting that what we might perceive as stress may be experienced quite differently to another person, so just because we get stressed by a particular issue or situation, such as with public speaking, doesn't mean that everyone else will too. Some might find public speaking energising, motivating and positively challenging. So it's not necessarily to look out for the issues or situations that can be sources of stress (though it's good to be alert to these) rather it's to have an empathic awareness of others so you can assess how someone else is coping.

We experience stress when we perceive that the demands placed upon us exceed our ability to cope. Central to this definition is the element of perception. To perceive something is to bring it into our conscious awareness. This means that a realisation may form in the unconsciousness, until we become aware of it. Or our awareness of something may oscillate along this conscious/unconscious continuum. This is why it can be difficult to be aware if we are stressed; sometimes we are not consciously aware of it.

A key indicator is a change which you notice in the other. There is something different about them or they are doing something different. This could be related to their behaviour, how they are communicating, a change to their dress or hygiene, a change in punctuality, a change in concentration or productivity. It might be subtle or obvious. But it's a change nonetheless.

Presenteeism is when someone is present at work, but not productive, a sort of sickness presence. The lights are on but nobody's home. This can be a sign of stress but it might mask other issues, such as a malaise or apathy towards work, poor workplace relationships, issues at home, mental health issues, lack of motivation, inspiration and aspiration or other problems at work. Absence can be more visible and pronounced and any trends, such as always being off on a Monday, could indicate issues of stress; they can't face the start of the week or there are problems at home.

Most people who experience stress remain at work and get on with it. But it can have an inhibiting impact on their work and, as a result, any knock-on effect on other team members. Stress can emerge from a multitude of mini-stresses which have not been effectively managed or resolved, yet they lurk in the background and snap out when least expected.

If people are stressed and struggle to contain their responses to it, they can find themselves projecting or ventilating their angst in unusual or innocuous ways. We hold all this pent-up stress energy and suddenly a spark ignites it and we kick out. Consider someone suppressing their cauldron of stress and then driving home, and suddenly becoming aware of a persistent rattle in the car somewhere. This innocuous rattle could suddenly become the most annoying thing in the world, out of all proportion, as the person is projecting all their masked stresses into that little rattle. It's similar when people kick out at innocuous things or for little rational reasons; they're projecting their stresses into this focused, concentrated target.

Top Tips

Are you OK?

If you are unsure or clear about someone's stress, just go up to them and ask them if they are OK, along with something you have observed which may indicate that they are not. This empathic resonance will offer them reassurance and might enable them to confirm if they are or are not. If they are OK, great.

Can I help?

If they're not OK, sometimes a little guidance, advice or support is all that is required to share some of the load or pressure. If you can't help, think of someone who can.

Appetite and diet

A change in eating habits can indicate stress. Is the person eating more or less than usual, are you aware of significant weight loss or gain? Are they eating more unhealthy foods or snacks than normal?

Sleep hygiene

Tiredness, lack of sleep or even oversleep can signal stress or the start of a more concerning medical condition such as anxiety or depression. Our sleep can be disturbed by disruptive thoughts at night, which are irrational and emotional, probably because we lack the input of our logical mind to give us perspective during the day. If you don't have the resources to resolve a problem at night, what's the point of thinking about it?

Irritability and impatience

Someone who gets angry quickly or is subject to outbursts, when it's not like them, can be on the stress precipice. They may be taking it out on you, on others or themselves.

Concentration and decision-making

Reduced concentration and less effective decision-making are also hallmarks of stress. This will impact on productivity, affecting whole teams. It can also lead to accidents and mistakes.

Physical ailments

There are a host of physical stress indicators, such as headaches and nausea, back and neck pain, muscle tension and aches, indigestion and heart burn. Unless you're a seasoned medic, don't just assume this is a stress reaction which will pass, as it could be more serious. Just encourage them to get it checked out by their doctor who should be able to better diagnose the physical or psychological source.

Introvert/extrovert

People react to stress in odd ways. Sometimes you get folk who suddenly take on a change in their personality, becoming more extrovert when they are usually introvert, or introvert when they are usually more of an extrovert. Again, checking out how they are is the first option. Their response will determine what you say next.

Dysfunctional coping

A range of coping mechanisms can help moderate or ease symptoms of stress, but can trigger other issues. Are they self-medicating with alcohol, or increasing their reliance on prescription drugs, or smoking more or using illegal drugs?

Action Plan 20: Stress Indicator Tool

Any of the following indicators may signify stress in others (and self). Circle those which apply;

Physical/Bodily	Cognitive/Thinking	Behavioural/Doing	Emotional/Feelings
Indigestion/heartburn	Irrational thoughts	Outbursts	Tearful/emotional
Change in appetite	Negative thinking	Disorganised/late	Anger/aggression
Sleep pattern change	Poor concentration	Obsessive behaviours	Frustration
Headache/migraine	Poor decision-making	Twitching/fidgeting	Angst
Tiredness/fatigue	Confused thinking	Alcohol/smoking	Depression/low-mood
Palpitation/sweating	Loss of memory	Prescribed drugs/opiates	Anxiety/worries
Dizzy/unsteady	Distracted	Illegal drugs	Irritation
Back/neck tension	Hopelessness	Avoiding people	Panic attacks
Muscle ache/pain	Helplessness	Unstructured	Mood changes

Stress is not a medical condition; however, if not addressed over time, symptoms of stress can trigger mental and physical health issues such as anxiety or depression, as well as physical pain and ailments.

Please consult with a medical doctor if you have concerns about your health.

If you have concerns about someone, please encourage them to consult with their doctor.

Section II

Personal and Family Life Management

21

Relationship MOT

Spotlight

An 'MOT' refers to the UK Ministry of Transport's (MOT) test carried out on all vehicles, currently over three years old, to check roadworthiness. An MOT is colloquially referred to as an 'annual check-up'.

And that's exactly how we refer to a 'Relationship MOT', an annual check-up. The start of most relationships involve a feisty mix of passion and emotion as we get to know each other and determine our compatibility. And somehow we begin to settle into a routine and structure of sharedness and togetherness, finding a way to retain some independence in a relationship or interdependence. We adapt our roles and responsibilities and find ways to compromise and share.

We might consider we have a good, strong relationship and that's great. As the dust settles, routines, structures, behaviours and habits form as we establish a norm and way of being together. New Year celebrations often focus on giving a nod to the things that happened in the departing year and looking forward to or making plans for the year ahead. But few of us do this with our relationships, and why not? How important is your relationship to you?

We deserve it to each other to assess and review how things are going. Are we sufficiently content and happy with our lot, or are there some niggles which are getting in the way? There's no such thing as a perfect relationship. We'll get annoyed, frustrated, angered, riled and vexed by each other now and again, and this is probably a healthy blow out, or a way we ventilate and express our emotions. We'll quarrel, argue, bicker and squabble (hopefully not all at once or all the time) but somehow, we usually just regroup and move on back into the healthy zone.

And usually we are quite good at 'pressing buttons' in each other, which refers to those little things that get on the nerves or annoy our partner, and we use them to just add an ounce of intent when we're wanting to provoke a particular response. It's like a relational sparring.

There can also be more hidden complexities that impact our relationships, predominantly based on our personalities and upbringing. We may be anchored by traumas from the pasts, ways in which we have been affected by different life experiences or the actions or emotional lives of our parents, family and friends.

Our past relationships will also influence our current relationship: decisions we have taken, mistakes we have made, actions we have regretted and poor choices made. We may have emotional 'baggage' weighing down on us. Well-worn behaviours, sticky habits or life scripts will all shape and define who we are today. But they don't need to inhibit us or reduce the potential for happiness. We just need to deal with them, get some meaning, closure and move on. The past is always the past; it can't be undone but we can learn to understand its influence and come to terms with it.

Our present lives will introduce periods when we are stressed or can't cope. Or work issues will preoccupy our thoughts and minds and we'll bring that back home into our relationships. When things worry us, we often need to talk … and our partner is the one we probably need to talk to most.

Top Tips

Smell the coffee
As we busy ourselves in our waking hours, through work, routine and structure, we often lose sight of what's right in front of us. Appreciate your partner, enjoy them, be with them, love them. Rediscover their smell, their fragrance, their sense of humour, their 'heart'.

Dialogue
Talking with your partner (not TO them) is one of the best ways of communicating the good, the bad and the ugly of your relationship so it is a two-way process. It's not always easy but sometimes it's necessary. Any form of dialogue and conversation is better than none.

Appreciation
Don't take your partner or your relationship for granted. Things can and do change, not necessarily the way we intended. We have accidents and illnesses, and tough times roll in and bad things happen. Appreciate what you have and savour.

Intimacy and sex
Apart from dismal robotic biology lessons at school, most have never been taught how to be intimate or how to have a healthy sex life. Explore and experiment and find what is right and healthy for both of you. Maybe that's all part of the fun? Seek professional help if things are not working out as this is an important part of your relationship which may need some attention, especially if you are not matched in 'sexual appetite'.

Conflicts
How do you manage or deal with disagreements? You'll always have occasions when you argue or bicker or squabble. What you disagree about possibly matters less than your mutual capacity to manage and resolve the situation.

Influence of others

We often underestimate how much impact other people have on our relationship; friends, family, parents, colleagues and so on. Do they help or hinder yours?

Past emotional baggage

Most of us have had past relationships, traumas or tough experiences which still affect us and can get in the way of our relationship. It's your responsibility (not your partner's) to find a way to deal with this. Get professional help if necessary with a therapist or coach. Doing nothing doesn't help.

Action Plan 21: Relationship MOT Model[1]

Work through the following questions with your partner, first individually, then discuss with them your and their responses. There's no right or wrong answer. There are some leading, quite personal questions; just write what you feel comfortable with. You might have quite different responses; that's OK. Use it as an opportunity to explore how you can enjoy making improvements for your relationship together.

1. What do you hope to gain from a Relationship MOT?

2. How well do you communicate with each other?

3. How do you spend sufficient quality time with each other?

4. How do you give each other the independence and personal space you require?

5. How happy are you with the intimacy between you?

---

[1] With thanks to Dorrit Prichard (Counsellor) for discussions in 2005 which led to the development of the Relationship MOT.

6. How happy are you with your sexual relationship?

7. How are you able to deal with and manage conflicts and disagreements when they occur?

8. How assertive are you in being able to clarify needs that are important to you?

9. Which of your emotional 'buttons' does your partner press and how and why does this happen?

10. How committed are you to each other?

11. How do you demonstrate your love for your partner?

12. To what degree do you trust your partner?

13. What were the things which attracted you to your partner initially?

14. What are the five most attractive qualities of your partner to you?

15. What is the least attractive quality of your partner to you?

16. What past emotional baggage do you carry which impacts your current relationship?

17. Can you identify any past emotional baggage your partner carries which affects the relationship?

18. If there's one thing you can do to improve your relationship what is it?

19. What do you take for granted about your partner?

20. What do you take for granted in your relationship?

21. How have your families affected your relationship?

22. How have friends affected your relationship?

23. How has your work affected your relationship?

24. How have work colleagues impacted your relationship?

25. How are you able to manage money and financial issues and is this OK for you?

26. To what degree do you share domestic responsibilities and is this OK for you?

27. How do children impact your relationship?

28. What future events (work, family, parties etc.) might impact your relationship?

29. How do you support and encourage each other?

30. What is the best way you can express your love to your partner taking into account what they respond to?

22

When Relationships End

Spotlight

It's always sad when a relationship fails, though sometimes this is necessary and the best thing for at least one of us. We engage in partnerships because we have a belief they will work. No one really goes into a relationship thinking or wanting it to fail. We genuinely hope, pray and maybe dream that it'll work out, it'll be great for us.

But it hasn't or didn't. It can feel devastating, heart breaking and rock us to our core. It can feel a very strong loss, like a bereavement. We have lost someone, something and part of ourselves. At the time, when it happens, it can feel like nothing will ever be the same again. Everything has changed.

As relationships involve two unique individual human beings, we are all different; different wants and needs, personalities and identities, hopes and dreams, motivated and inspired by different things. There's usually one person who feels they are more hurt than the other when it fails, though this can ebb and flow, and depends on our coping skills and resilience as well as the reason why the relationship ended.

There's always a reason why a relationship breaks down; things done and said, or things that were not said and not done which should have been. There might be rational reasons or irrational ones. And at some point there will be a sense of blame and guilt thrown into the mix. How could it have happened? How could it have happened to us, to me?

Making sense of it all can be complex. It can seem obvious and make complete sense or seem totally unreal and make no sense what so ever. Understanding what happened is part of the process of recovery, though in some cases we may never understand. For instance, if someone says they have 'fallen out of love' what does this really mean? How can someone fall OUT of love? In as much as we don't know why people fall IN love, perhaps the same applies the other way too. Or someone walks out of a relationship and simply never comes back. No explanation, no reason.

Stubbornness is often a primal trigger or cause. We simply stick our heels in and do not budge on an issue. No negotiation. No compromise. A gulf opens up that becomes difficult to bridge and agreement and reconciliation appear impossible. And then we decide that's it. End of. This 'pride factor' is the doom of many relationships, yet what does it achieve? Nothing. It is usually the nail in the coffin of a relationship.

Like a bereavement, we tend to go through a transitional process over a period of time. There's no real rule as to how long this takes, as we all need a different amount of time. It can range from days to years. We will never forget the relationship, but in time, it will diminish in our minds and the memories will fade.

Top Tips

TLC
The first thing you can do is look after yourself. Whatever has happened, you deserve it to yourself to give yourself the nourishment, support and space to work through everything.

Reconciliation?
Sometimes a relationship is not quite over when it might otherwise seem so. OK, you've had a massive falling out, but is it worth looking for that glimmer of compromise and hope? Is it not worth chancing it? Is

there anything to lose? So what if you have to eat a bit of humble pie by accepting that you were wrong or need to apologise?

Compatibility

Maybe you both were simply not compatible enough. It happens. There might have been a lot that worked out between you, and you maybe had some great times, but perhaps this was not enough. It takes a lot to really find someone we can live with for the rest of our lives.

Forgiveness

Relationships end with bucketfuls of guilt, blame, remorse and regret. It's heavy stuff and weighs deep on us. Work towards a position when you can forgive … forgive yourself, forgive your partner, forgive yourself for the wasted months or years. You may never forget the relationship but you can learn to forgive, and in so doing you will release yourself from some of the anchors of guilt, blame, remorse and regret. Also, in the future you may come to realise that nothing is totally wasted and that you will have learnt something from it.

Feeling down

It's likely you will slide into a pit of sadness and low-mood. Sometimes this is a normal part of the coping process and you need a bit of 'time out' to gather your thoughts and emotions, make sense of things and have some space to yourself. If you find this is lasting longer than a month or so, do check this out with your doctor just in case this is affecting your mental health more adversely.

Connections

You might want, and need, a period on your own to regroup and re-energise but don't isolate yourself for too long or unnecessarily. We all need contact with others, including friends and family. Build, create or find a network of people who can offer you the support, distraction or engagement you need.

Positivity

When things break down, the last thing you want to hear about is someone suggesting you think positively. But why not? You need to engage with and work through the relationship loss and you should get through it in the end. But you still deserve positivity in your life. Find what you can where you can. It's not disingenuous or disrespectful to have moments of positivity and enjoyment.

Opportunity

As one door closes, another one often opens. With an ending comes the opportunity of a new beginning. Keep your options open and your radar tuned to choices, events, people and experiences.

Healthy lifestyle

Maintain a healthy diet and sleep and rest well. When you feel down and lethargic, suitable exercise can help. It can pump nature's own 'feel-good endorphin' hormones round you and might encourage you to connect with the outside world.

Action Plan 22: Post-relationship Transitional Model

This model gives you an idea of the stages you may experience as you work through getting over the loss of your relationship. It may help to understand the different stages you may encounter as a normal part of 'moving on'.

Ending Zone	Transition Zone	Moving on Zone
Anxiety/Fear	Depression/Low mood	Acceptance
Blame	Anger	Exploration
Saying goodbye	Guilt/Remorse/Regret	Positivity
Hurt/Pain/Sadness	Purgatory/Empty place	Review
Letting Go	Reassessment	Cleansing/Purifying
Loss	Alternating moods	Opportunities
Change to self-image	Unsettlement	Options/Choices

→----------------------→ TIME →----------------------→

23

Anxiety Management

Spotlight

We don't want to get rid of all anxiety. It's an important human emotion which alerts us to feelings of threat, risk and danger. Often it's associated with the 'fight or flight' response where our body prepares itself to flee from or fight against a threat. It's a crucial warning mechanism and we need it. This chapter therefore seeks to normalise a degree of anxiety so that we learn to adjudicate, regulate or choose how to react to an anxiety-provoking situation.

But sometimes we can find that we feel anxious more times than the 'threat warning' is necessary. We can live in a more routine or permanent state of anxiety, on edge and constantly alert. This provides an inaccurate or skewed perception of the threat and fails to be utilised when it really matters. We can feel anxious about almost anything and become preoccupied by worries and fears.

In most cases we are over-exaggerating the threat and catastrophising about the worst case scenario. We spend inordinate, inappropriate and unnecessary energy and time hooking into concerns which just go round and round in circles and never seem to resolve themselves.

We can become restless and fidgety, irritable and angst ridden, have flushed faces and sweaty palms, feel light-headed or prone to headaches, think the worst and out of proportion to the threat. All these behavioural, psychological and physical responses merge into one massive anxiety tsunami. We feel like we will explode. We might react and kick out or hole up into a cocoon and socially isolate ourselves. These responses further feed the anxiety time bomb.

How we end up like this can be a combination of variables; how we have coped with anxiety in the past (or not); life events and crisis situations; attitudes and behaviours of our parents, family and friends; modelling from how others respond to anxiety; our health, fitness, diet and lifestyle behaviours; and scripts or habits we have adopted, and learnt to normalise, over time.

But it doesn't have to be like this. It's not about getting rid of all anxiety, but learning to accept, appreciate and benefit from the 'good' or normal anxiety and training ourselves not to reach out for the unhealthy and unproductive anxiety when we really don't need it, when it serves no purpose.

Final point to note: if your anxiety is not temporary or is affecting your normal level of functioning especially if you are experiencing panic attacks, it is worth checking this out with your doctor. Medication is not necessarily a long-term solution (when finding the root causes for anxiety might be), but it may help in the short term and can be best used in combination with psychological support.

Top Tips

Get a grip on reality

Once you are in a calm state, reflect on a recent period of anxiety you endured. To what degree was your response or reaction appropriate to the real threat which existed? Write down what you believe was applicable and what was excessive or over the top.

Embrace 'good' anxiety

Appreciate and embrace when anxiety served you well, for instance, did a degree of anxiety help you focus on, or motivate you at, a public speaking event, or a social situation or an exam or interview?

You are not alone
Know, hear and appreciate that many people feel anxious in common situations when you do too. Most people feel anxious in new social situations or when speaking in public or at interviews. If you don't believe this, ask your friends or family. Knowing it's normal for them too might normalise it for you.

Negate negative thinking
Sometimes there's a little voice inside us nipping away with negative thoughts; criticising, blaming and reprimanding us for things we have or haven't done. These can fuel our anxiety monster with unhelpful fears and worries. Challenge these negative thoughts so they don't take hold.

Stay in the present
Lots of anxiety is associated with the future: things that have not yet happened and may never happen. Or it might be linked to things from the past. We can't change the past and we can't necessarily control the future. So what's the point in worrying about the past or the future? But we can control and change the here and now. What can you change in terms of what you can do, think or feel now? Stay mindful and in the moment.

Action stations
Sometimes, the mere act of doing something different in the moment can take you out of your anxious state. Distract yourself; go for a walk, listen to some music, read a book, learn something new, sing a song, get into a hobby or interest, go shopping, eat something ... anything.

Catastrophe-city
Often we legitimise worrying about the worst case scenario as we convince ourselves that this helps us prepare for every eventuality. But what a waste of time and effort, especially when you consider the remote possibility of this actually happening. Could you spend some of this time enjoying life more?

Reconceptualise anxiety
You need a new and different relationship with anxiety. Learn to feel the benefit of 'good' anxiety, where it serves you well and how it may help

to motivate, inspire and encourage you. But also differentiate this with 'bad' anxiety, where it serves no purpose. When you can do this you can choose to 'be' anxious, or not.

Perfectionism

The vicious circle of perfectionism is that we strive to achieve a perpetual impossible high and by failing to reach it we release an anxiety which needs us to reach that impossible high. Learn to accept a reality which is achievable, realistic and more genuine, which takes the pressure off and shuts the door on the anxiety driver.

Action Plan 23: Ten-Minute Rapid Relaxation Technique

In a quiet, warm place, lie or sit, and then close your eyes.

Take about four seconds to breathe in slowly through your nose, hold it for another four, then breathe out slowly through your mouth for another four seconds, feeling the tension ease out of your body.

Repeat this six or so times, feeling the stress leave your body and your heart rate lowering as you enter a state of relaxation.

Inhale, hold, then exhale.

Focus your attention on your toes and feet, lightly and slowly tensing them, then relaxing them, feeling the tension ease. Tense when you inhale, relax the tension as you exhale.

Feel the muscles around your feet, on the soles, around your ankles, keeping up with the slow relaxed breathing; tense, then relax as you breathe out.

Focus on your calf muscles and around your lower leg, tense, breathe in, then release and breathe out. Then move up to your knees, the back of your knees, tense and relax.

Then to the muscles in your thighs, tense and breathe in, pause, then relax and breathe out, feeling the tension envelope all of your legs.

Then move to your buttocks, tensing, then relaxing, keeping the same four second rule to your breathing and feeling the stress leave your body.

Feel your lower back, where tension often exists, then over to your stomach, tense and relax, arch your back slightly, where this is comfortable, tense and relax. Then feel the pectorals on your chest, breathe in, pause and relax as you breathe out and relax.

Clench and release your fists, moving up your arms, inhaling, pausing, then exhaling.

Up to your shoulders including your shoulder blade; feeling the tension float away as you tense, breathe in, pause, then relax and breathe out.

Then feel the area around your neck and the back of your head. Feel the tension ease away. Then surrounding your head; your ears, jaw, cheeks and nose; breathe in, pause, then exhale.

Finally, focus in on your forehead and the central area just above the bridge of your nose. Feel the relaxation centring into your head, grounding you in a blanket of comfort.

Keep the breathing going, in for four, pause for four, out for four, feeling your whole body stress-free and in a state of deep relaxation.

When you are ready, open your eyes and savour how good you feel.

24

Living with Depression

Spotlight

It is very common to feel low, or down, or sad from time to time, usually in response to a difficult or stressful situation. It is often the body's way of retreating, protecting or cocooning itself from the issue of concern. Perhaps we have experienced some considerable disappointment, distress, trauma, shock, discontentment, despondency or dismay. Or it might relate to feelings of loss, associated with a relationship break-up, redundancy, going bankrupt or the death of a loved one.

The way in which we grieve and deal with loss is unique for each of us, but the feelings of sadness usually recede over time as we recover. Significant loss can push us into a depression, particularly when the feelings of low mood last for a long time and become debilitating. However, there is a difference between grief and depression. Those grieving find their sadness comes and goes and they can still have periods when they feel positive. Depression tends to be a more chronic sadness that affects sufferers on a much more constant and severe basis.

Causes of depression are often associated with medical issues, such as a family history of depression, body and brain chemistry and hormonal changes (pregnancy, menopause, thyroid issues etc.). But there are also further risk factors, including abuse of alcohol and use of recreational drugs; responses to traumatic or critical incidents; physical, psychological and sexual abuse and serious or chronic illness, pain or injury.

Symptoms of depression can include loss of interest in normal pleasures; apathy; irritability and frustration; changes in weight, diet, energy levels and sleep patterns; anxiety and agitation; reduced concentration and productivity; back and neck pain and, potentially, suicidal thoughts.

A combination of all these factors can isolate us from others, stop us doing the things we used to do, make it difficult to function normally and leave us in periods of complete inactivity. These further feed the depression cycle and weigh us down further.

We all react in unique ways; physically, psychologically, emotionally, socially, culturally and environmentally, which makes the identification of causes, consequences and cures of depression different and difficult. In most cases, it is worth checking this out with your doctor. You are in charge of you, but doctors can assist with your recovery. Whilst potentially diagnosing for various forms of depression, they can also rule out other physical illness which can replicate the symptoms of depression.

Prescription medication could help you; anti-depressants don't tend to change your mood excessively, rather they are often described as 'mood stabilisers', taking you from that pit of depression to a more manageable level. A combination of anti-depressants and talking therapy plus exercise can be a successful mix of treatment.

But there are things you can do, whether you are experiencing sadness, loss, grief, depression or a cocktail of all of these.

Top Tips

Talk to doc
Make an appointment to see a doctor. They may be able to diagnose what is wrong, as well as ruling out any physical issues.

Is there a cause?
Maybe your feelings of depression are associated with an event in the past? Can you work out when you started feeling down and what was

happening then? Once you know a possible source, you may be better able to work through making sense of that trigger issue.

Exercise and fitness

Physical exercise is known to be a mood enhancer through releasing the body's natural endorphins. If you exercise with others, particularly with team sports and activities, you also gain social contact, which can also improve mood and reduce isolation and loneliness.

Sleep, diet and relaxation

If your sleeping is impaired, try guided meditation, relaxation exercises, a warm detoxifying drink at night, a bath, reading or natural herbal sleeping remedies, but check with your doctor what is suitable. Keep meals regular and have a healthy varied diet; eat small and regular if you struggle to eat large meals. And relax. Social media is not necessarily relaxing, and the blue screen on devices can impair sleep and impact mood.

Alcohol and recreational drugs

Alcohol is a depressant and drugs can trigger different mood and psychological conditions. They might feel like mood enhancers, take you out of a depressive void and elevate you to an escapist place of peace, but it doesn't last; it's only temporary, and you'll feel much worse than before.

Job and work

It might seem counter-intuitive when you're laid out with depressive symptoms, but going to work creates routine and structure, can give us purpose and meaning, pays the bills, gives us social contact, can inspire, enthuse and motivate … all antidotes to feelings of sadness and low mood. Work can be good for our mental health, or, putting it another way, being unemployed or without work or purpose can feed in to a declining mental health condition.

Counselling and therapy

Talking therapies can provide an opportunity to talk through how your low mood or depression affects you, coming to terms with it or looking for causes and exploring potential solutions. Knowing you are not alone helps too. Depression groups meet up to offer support, camaraderie and companionship to those experiencing depression.

Self-validation

A final, if contentious, Top Tip, proposes that in some cases depression serves a function or meets a behavioural need in some people (certainly not everyone with depression), thereby validating its persistent existence. This might be due to the need for sympathy, pity or solace, or a need to be heard, noticed or appreciated. Negative thinking can also invite symptoms of depression. If you experience low mood, especially without a clear cause, do you have a choice? Think about it.

Action Plan 24: Non-activity Spiral of Depression Model

A vicious circle can emerge involving activity and depression.

You feel depressed, which saps your energy and triggers your low mood, which decreases your inclination for activity, which increases lethargy, apathy, plus feelings of hopelessness and guilt, which feed into the depression voice, which saps your energy ... and so on.

Whereas increasing activity gives you more energy, which makes you feel more positive and hopeful, which reduces the severity of the depression, which gives you greater energy and motivation, which encourages you to do more activity, which gives you more energy ... and so on.

Write down five enjoyable activities you can do which are feasible, practical and realistic.

Write down WHAT you will do—be specific, WHEN you will do it—so you nail down a time to commit to, HOW you will do it—so you consider the actions necessary to do it and WHY—to reinforce the reason why you enjoy the activity and want to do it.

1. I will (what)   _____

   on (when)   _____

   by (how)   _____

   because (why)   _____

2. I will (what) _____

   on (when) _____

   by (how) _____

   because (why) _____

3. I will (what) _____

   on (when) _____

   by (how) _____

   because (why) _____

4. I will (what) _____

   on (when) _____

   by (how) _____

   because (why) _____

5. I will (what) _____

   on (when) _____

   by (how) _____

   because (why) _____

WHY is possibly the most important question/answer as this will create your passion, meaning and purpose for your intention; it's the engine behind your momentum of enthusiasm.

25

Changing Negative-Thinking Patterns

Spotlight

There are many reasons why we think negatively. We may have low self-worth, low self-confidence or low self-esteem; we might be self-critical or self-blaming; we could have depression or a mental or physical health condition; or it might be a learned behaviour habit or life script.

Thinking negatively comes in many shapes and sizes, but often follows a series of patterns.

All-or-nothing thinking is where we fail to see anything other than a polarised view; we either chose to do something right or not at all. There is no grey area in between or ambiguity for maybe choosing to do something well, or pretty good; 'if I don't get a first class honours degree, I'm useless'.

Some thinking is selective, where we pay attention only to the evidence that serves us at the time, so we might choose to focus on our failures and weaknesses, rather than successes and strengths; 'That presentation I gave last month was the worst I've ever given, so they'll always be as bad as that'. Similarly we choose to ignore the good things and disqualify the positives; such as 'the presentation we gave the month before last which was brilliant'.

We might overgeneralise, thinking that 'everything's a nightmare', 'nothing goes right' or 'I'm always useless'. Or we might catastrophise and blow things out of proportion; 'If I don't get that job, I will never find any work again' or 'If I am not in a relationship, I can't be happy'.

There's also the potential to jump to the wrong conclusion using skewed or misguided thinking, such as believing we know what others are thinking, and assuming it is bad; 'they hate me' or we think we can predict the future, 'I won't get the job because the interview questions will be very unfair'.

It might be that our emotional reasoning misdirects our thinking, so because we feel something, we believe it to be true; 'I feel lonely, therefore I am unlovable' or 'I didn't get the job, so I'm useless'. This resonates with negative labelling, making a judgement or opinion about ourselves or others; 'I'm so incompetent and worthless' or 'I'm just stupid'.

A final negative-thinking pattern involves the inappropriate blaming of self or others, or the misappropriation of responsibility; 'we lost that contract because I was on the team, even though I was away for the pitch which lost it' or 'How dare you accuse me of bullying behaviour, I am simply asserting myself as my rights trump everyone else's'.

And there are other negative-thinking patterns which feed off the tributaries of the above. We usually know when they are happening. The problem is that we don't always know what to do in the heat of the moment. Often this is because we are in such a spiral or hurricane that we just lock ourselves out of any chance of a solution; we can't see the wood for the trees.

Top Tips

Body language

Sometimes we hold ourselves in a self-fulfilling manner, so if we feel down or negative, we slouch or stoop. Hold yourself tall and firm, chest out, head held high. Breathe in confidently, smile genuinely.

Distraction with action

You can change your negative thinking by changing your situation, which means doing something differently; listen to music, read a book, write a letter, have a bath, go for a walk, drink water, and so on.

Change the situation
If your negativity is fuelled by the people around you or the company you keep, get out of that environment and reconsider whether you can resist returning to those mongers of doom.

Reality check
Over-exaggeration and catastrophising can be kept in check by taking a reality check of the situation. Consider the real facts, not the fears. What is the evidence or proof?

Guided meditation
Get some psychological and emotional grounding by tuning into a 20 minutes or so of guided meditation to calm your breathing, de-stress your muscles and relax your body, mind and soul. There are many free 'tracks' on the internet.

Find your relaxation sensation
We all relax and chill out in different ways. What suits you and your circumstances? It might be a game of darts down the pub, walking round the block, a candle-lit bath, cooking a meal for a loved one, listening to a piece of classical music, knitting, building model aeroplanes and so on.

Semantics
Try changing the words about your negative thinking; so 'that public speaking presentation was a complete failure, and so am I' could be rephrased as 'there were some challenging moments in that talk, but I know where I went wrong and I'll be better next time'.

Stay mindful
A lot of negative thinking can be associated with things that have happened in the past—which you can't change—or worries about things which might happen in the future—which you can't control. Either way, there's usually nothing you can do, so negative thinking is pointless and serves no function or purpose. Stay with the 'here and now' and you stay with reality.

Health and fitness

Having a healthy mind stems from a healthy body and vice versa, which requires you to exercise in a manner which is appropriate for you, getting enough quality sleep and rest, and eating a balanced healthy diet.

Write on

If you are plagued by persistent negative thoughts, write down why and when you have them or what purpose they are serving or a way to define how you are experiencing them. Once you have expressed your negativity on paper, burn it (safely) or flush it down the toilet (environmentally). This mimics the action of flushing or washing away, or burning up your negativity.

Action Plan 25: Cognitive-Behavioural Therapy (CBT) Thought Record

Reflect on a recent event or situation when you were thinking negatively.

Use the Thought Record, below, to challenge your negative thinking and move to a more self-accepting and flexible positive belief about yourself.

A therapist experienced in CBT may be able to help you apply this approach to your life.

Changing Negative-Thinking Patterns

Situation	Emotion or feeling	Negative thought	Evidence which supports the negative thought	Evidence which does not support the negative thought	Alternative thoughts	Emotion or feeling
What was happening?	What was your primary emotion?	What was your primary negative thought?	What facts support this negative thought?	What facts suggest this negative thought is not true all of the time?	Write a new thought based on the evidence for and against the original thought	How do you feel about the situation now?

26

Supporting Elderly Dependents

Spotlight

Society is ageing as healthier living and advances in medicine prolong our lives. But it doesn't stop us from ageing. We all grow old and with this our mental and physical faculties will decline and trigger a series of often interconnected limitations. As much as possible, we want to remain independent and capable. But most of us will reach a point when we will become more dependent and incapable.

In the United Kingdom, between 1976 and 2016 there was a 3.8 percentage point increase in the proportion of people aged 65 and over. However, it is projected to continue to grow to nearly a quarter of the population by 2046 (Overview of the UK population: July 2017. Office for National Statistics.)

Demands on health and social care provision will have a huge impact on the capabilities of societies to provide suitable and appropriate support. Government policy and local authority provision together with funding criteria will determine access to public and private resources.

Closer to home, our respective family make-ups will influence how we are able to, or not able to, support those who age and require our support. The elderly can sometimes be regarded as a forgotten generation, as we prioritise our own immediate family demands together with balancing the pressures of work and earning a living.

Most of us don't sufficiently factor in the fact that we may have ageing family members who will need, or at least want, our support. What we can and do offer may be different to expectations. It can be a really tough balance to find with no easy compromises.

Another way of looking at it is considering our situation when we reach our 70s, 80s or 90s. How might our brains and bodies be functioning? Can we look after ourselves fully or partially, or might we need 24-hour care? Who's going to give us privacy, dignity and respect during any infirmity? Who's going to look after us? Who's going to talk to us? Who's going to bother about us?

What does ageing mean to us? For some of us it might mean adjusting to limitations of body and mind. Or of reaching a point when we may not achieve the life ambitions we sought. Of settling with what has passed and adapting to the present, aware there could be a limited future ahead.

But it's not all doom and gloom. It can also be about celebrating their life. Revelling in the highs and lows and appreciating the rich depths of experiencing, enjoying the reflective moments of achievements and successes but also appreciating the struggles, crisis situations and traumas along the way.

It might also give them a chance to consider their own periods of resilience, as they overcame struggles and grew to learn from those experiences and maybe become a better person for it. Often underappreciated is the wealth of knowledge, wisdom and maturity that comes with old age. How can they best nurture and cherish this goldmine and contribute this to the wider good in society?

We spend so much time re-learning the same old things and reinventing the wheel, when a perfectly good wheel already exists. Do we not learn anything? We can from the elderly. And they can learn from us too.

Top Tips

Need to know

You're probably not a mind reader. But you have to understand what the needs are for the elderly person. What is it they need or want, and why? What's important to them? It could be little but significant. Assumptions can lead to glaring misunderstandings. Ask them.

Practical advice

Do you need to find legal, consumer or financial advice for the elderly person and would it help or hinder to accompany them? There's a balance about privacy, confidentiality and understanding.

Health needs

Most of us don't like to admit it when our bodies start to falter. Similarly, would it help or hinder to accompany them to the doctor or for a medical appointment?

Mortality

Do you need to have 'the conversation' about death and dying or what are their wishes for the future? Even if it's just about asking that very question. Better to ask and get a polite (or otherwise) refusal than to regret not having asked. Additionally, not having a Will is a big problem for those left behind and can cause family conflict and financial hardship, so it is a prudent topic to discuss.

Regression

There can be a sense of role reversing, of the parent becoming the child and the child stepping up to become the parent. Stay in the adult-adult zone with them and expect to be psychologically met as an adult.

Needs analysis

Needs can change quickly physically and psychologically so you need to maintain an up-to-date needs audit; what are the needs and what are the wants? Why and how have these changed? Be aware of preventative steps in the home such as removing trip hazards or putting in hand rails; an older person can take much longer to recover from broken bones.

Accept the reality of change

As circumstances and needs change, there comes a realisation on all sides, that things are not going to be the same ever again. Things have changed for good. It won't be like before. It's about adapting to, and accommodating, the new way however good or challenging this may be.

Frustration

As we age, our brains take longer to process thoughts, memories and decisions. We might become forgetful. This can all get hugely frustrating and feel like a curse of ageing. It can contribute to feelings of low self-worth and negative criticism and blame. You might not be able to do anything about this, but you can empathise with any frustrations. Perhaps unusually, some people find a sense of humour can help here.

Emotional volatility

Not everyone accepts the changes associated with ageing. They might have been the 'strong one', but now they're the 'weak one'. Independence changes to dependence. Anticipate strong feelings, emotional outbursts, anger and aggression. It's not personal even if it might feel like it.

Depression

Depression is common in the elderly and often goes undiagnosed. Moodiness and irritability might mask symptoms of depression.

Isolation

The elderly can be prone to loneliness and isolation, particularly if they live on their own. How can you help to reach out, connect and engage better or build a Dream Team of people around them?

Alcohol

With less to get up for in the morning or with ailments, low-mood and diminishing capabilities, there may be an increasing reliance on alcohol as a self-medicating aid. This can also be the result of long-term unrecognised alcoholism.

Access to support

Knowing that there is help and support as and when it is needed can offer much reassurance. Help to identify a 'Dream-Team' of key individuals, resources, health-care providers, community resources, support agencies and also family and friends who can be contacted for different needs.

Action Plan 26: Needs Audit for Elderly Dependents

Whilst each situation is unique in terms of needs and resources, the following template can act as a routine assessment of support needs in order to identify how these can be met by whom.

✓

- ☐ 'Messages'; routine shopping for basic and regular foodstuffs, perishables and cleaning products
- ☐ Occasional shopping for clothes, shoes, home furnishings and so on
- ☐ Housework; cleaning, tidying, ironing, gardening and so on
- ☐ Cooking, food preparation, dietary needs and healthy eating
- ☐ Healthcare needs including prescriptions and home modifications
- ☐ Transportation needs; getting around, public transport, lifts and so on.
- ☐ Hygiene and cleanliness; attending to basics, bathing, showering, toileting and so on.
- ☐ Entertainment and fun; activities, interests, social engagement and connecting with others
- ☐ Exercise and physical fitness, at home or with others
- ☐ DIY tasks; changing lightbulbs, fixing or repairing broken things and odd jobs about the home
- ☐ Safety; removing trip hazards and fitting aids such as hand rails or rubber mats in a bathroom

27

Bereavement and Loss

Spotlight

Bereavement is the state or action of being deprived of or losing something or someone. It is a very unique and personal experience. Any form of loss can be painful and summon up complex, unaccustomed and competing emotions, feelings and thoughts.

How we cope with loss is influenced by our previous experience of loss, our upbringing and background, our current levels of pressure or stress, people support around us and our resilience. Some people find it preoccupies every waking thought, whilst others can compartmentalise and focus on other distractions. Work can help provide a routine and structure, but others might find themselves very tearful and emotional, unable to concentrate or make decisions.

We can be locked into specific thoughts or memories, which may be happy (remembering a smile or a hug) or distressing (seeing the dead body). Or we might have floating and fleeting images, maybe of the person suddenly walking back into the room or hearing their voice. It could affect our sleeping, keeping us awake at night with nightmares, or impact on our diet, eating more or less than we usually do. Our energy levels could be affected as we find ourselves apathetic and lethargic, or we might find ourselves falling into a depression.

Or we might find ourselves lost in a sea of erratic thoughts and emotions, deeply sad one moment, and then numb the next, or raging with anger, then in a state of guilt and disbelief. It might seem odd, but these are all normal reactions to an abnormal event. Whilst death is not abnormal in itself, the circumstances and impact can be tragic or horrific and like nothing we have ever experienced before or imagined. One bereavement or loss is always different to another.

The process of grieving can take time to recover from, lasting anything from weeks, months and years. There's no firm time line. We may ebb and flow, with thoughts in our minds one minute, then no memory the next. People tend to become aware of recovery from bereavement when they are noticing that they are getting on with their lives more and thinking less of the person who has died. This is not about forgetting … you are likely never to forget them. Rather it's when you take back more control and start getting on with your life again, rather than being distracted and put off balance by the shock of the bereavement.

What is consistent, universal and shared is the fact that it hurts and can be excruciating at times, as if we will never recover or move on. But we usually do … in time, and this will change us in some way.

Top Tips

Multitude of emotions

Grieving triggers a succession of feelings and emotions. Some will seem familiar and make sense, such as feelings of sadness and pain. You might also feel angry, which might seem totally inappropriate, disrespectful and insensitive.

Self-care

You may not feel like it, but do look after yourself; attend to your health with a balanced diet, try to get the sleep you need, aim to carry on with some exercise and, when the time is appropriate, keep up with some social contact. If you find the situation intolerable and affecting your normal functioning, do go and get checked out by your doctor.

It's good to talk

Much of bereavement processing is trying to make sense of what has happened. Talking to a therapist, or a friend or family members can help you to find some clarity, though you may never get the answers you seek. Talking it out with someone is often more cathartic than internalising any pain and angst within you.

Stages of loss

Whatever the type of loss or bereavement, we often go through a series of stages, usually but not always, sequentially. Knowing what these stages are can help us understand our reactions and responses to loss. It can give meaning and understanding to our bereavement process.

The remainder of the 'Top Tips' which follow chart the phases or stages of grief:

Feeling shock, numbness and in denial

Very soon after the death or loss, you may experience a sense of shock, not really believing what has happened or that it has happened to you. You may experience a numbness, emptiness or void or deny what has happened. This can feel quite surreal, like you are floating above a reality which you are not connected with.

Feeling anger and resentment

You may find yourself angry and irritable. This might be directed at family, or friends, the hospital and carers or even the person who has died. Doing this can feel disrespectful and in itself contribute to further feelings of guilt and self-criticism. You may want to point the finger or blame people, to accuse them of incompetence or of not doing enough. You might even blame yourself.

Feeling sorrow, despair and guilt

After a funeral, wake, memorial or thanksgiving service, you might experience a very deep and intense period of sadness … the well-wishers have disappeared, the contact with people offering support might have dwindled and you will now face the stark reality of the situation, where the loss hits home, realising that the loss is permanent.

Feelings of depression, apathy and disconnection

The sadness of the reality can then shift into a more depressive stage, where you might isolate yourself from others and want to be on your own. This is a normal coping reaction, though it may also make you feel more lonely and isolated, which could exacerbate further the impact of loss.

Stage of acceptance, revival and reconnection

Soon, however, you will start to get on with your life more, find more enthusiasm and get your energy back, connecting with others and engaging with people again. You haven't forgotten the loss, you are simply focusing on you again. There will still be good days and bad days, happy days and sad days. This is about starting to accept and move on, getting on with your life.

Stage of transformation, growth and enlightenment

Some people find that after a bereavement or loss, they will start to re-evaluate their own sense of purpose or meaning, their values and aspirations. It's as if everything has changed slightly and can never be the same again. It gives you a period when you might get quite reflective; what does loss mean to you, how might you make changes in your life from now on. This final stage is reflective and can be transformational.

Stage of remembrance and thanksgiving

You will always remember what you have lost. You choose how you want to mark and respect your loss, when you do this and with whom. It can be something you want to do with family and friends, or alone. What you choose one year, might be different another. Do you reflect on the loss, or do you celebrate the impact … or both?

Action Plan 27: Stages of Loss Model[1]

Reflect on or pinpoint the stages of loss as you experience them.

Whilst you may find this passes sequentially, sometimes you might revert to an earlier stage or jump forward.

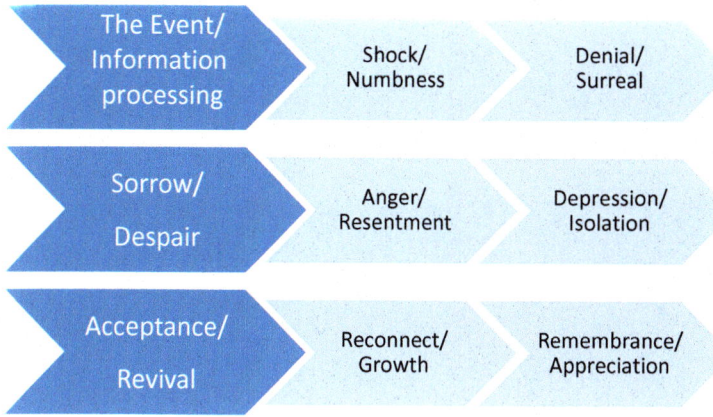

---

[1] This model is loosely adapted from the Kubler-Ross model's 'five stages of grief' (1969).

28

Stages in Life

Spotlight

Life can be strange. When we're young, we become fixated by wanting to appear older and then something happens. It's like a switch is flicked and for the rest of our lives we become fixated by wanting to appear younger!

When we're young, we don't think much about the future; that's too far away, and anyway we're more concerned with the present issues of how we're getting on at school or college, our friendships, our loves, our families and working out how to make sense of the world around us. And yet this is a continual issue. Throughout life, we'll still be concerned with family, relationships and probably still be looking to make sense of the world around us.

Life can be about a series of events, some planned, some unplanned. Our chapter on Life Cycle Events (Chap. 51) explores the losses and gains associated with different situations. Here, though, we touch more on the impacts of a series of sequential life stages which we will all experience. Each will have issues or conflicts, broad ambitions or opportunities, plus challenges or threats.

Sometimes we simply stumble into a new stage in life or we might reluctantly snake into it after time spent avoiding or fearing it. Either way, we usually don't have much choice. Provided we are blessed with good health and good luck, we transition through each life stage, one after the other.

Each stage gives us a new and different perspective on life … what has gone before, what is happening in the here and now and what confronts us ahead. And we will have built up a little more life experience, a little more maturity and hopefully a little more dexterity in our life management.

But it's also at the heart of resilience too, stepping from one life stage to the next as deftly as possible, transitioning from a previous sense of self to a newly evolving one. Our character, identity and personality change. This might be influenced by changes in jobs, friends, family dynamics, where we live, health and our relationships. It's a hefty matrix of variables which weave their own idiosyncratic mix of impacts and consequences, which in turn sets off a new train of events.

In many cases, blending into a new life stage offers the opportunity to reflect on learning and insight as our advancing maturity offers wisdom and worldliness. But it's not all so positive. We're going to be hitting psychological blocks or walls; we're going to experience life crisis issues; we'll have moments of horror, shock and terror; and we'll have powerful and emotional moments of sadness and low mood, plus fear, worry and anxiety.

Life is a journey. Not always a clear, unruffled journey, but a journey none the less. If we can appreciate and accept an unpredictable and foggy landscape in front of us, we can learn to adapt accordingly or at least tolerate the ambiguity which permeates throughout.

Top Tips

Embrace

We can't stop time. Each day we get that little bit closer to the next life stage. If you try to fight the unfightable you'll get frustrated and internally deconstruct. Let it all in and go with the flow.

Enjoy

With each and every stage, there are new opportunities and potentials which did not exist before. There's now a chance to enjoy this new lease of life. If you regard life stages as full of possibilities, then you'll find the possibilities.

Get attitude

Whilst each life stage presents a loss from the previous one, if you hanker after this loss you'll lose sight of the present. Keep up a positive mental attitude. Mourn the passing of change, if this helps, but celebrate your achievements and successes, as much as how you got through tough times too.

Grieve the losses

Each life stage introduces a new era but also creates a departure from or loss of a previous one. Reflect on, mark, appreciate and celebrate the time gone by and the stage departed. This will always remain part of you and your life experience. You've just moved on that little bit further.

Control

It's easy to feel you have no control of the passing of time. But bring in control by making active decisions; do things that forge change, connect with more or new people, enhance your creativity, focus on an appropriate work–life balance and instigate your new way of being.

People power

As we move through life's stages, our friendship networks evolve. Ditch those historical friendships that are destructive or unhelpful for you and invest in finding the right people who enhance and nourish your world.

Family

You can change your friends but you can't change your family. Yet you have a solidarity, connection and bond with family; nurture and develop those relationships. Be open and transparent, empathising with difficulties but asserting your own position. Family doesn't just have to be those closest; consider your cousins, distant relations—they're still connected to you by birth and may present less conflict and an inspiration, insight and depth into your wider work and personal worlds.

Health and fitness

While you can't change your family, you can change your lifestyle to one which is appropriately healthy. Find ways to enjoy a healthy diet, embrace exercise and fitness as a bodily reward rather than an effort, and delight in a sleep pattern which helps you wake refreshed and embracing the day.

Choose life

Choices give you options. Develop a choice strategy where you can sniff out options at every opportunity. This will inoculate you from feelings of being stuck in a rut or trapped in a metaphorical cage of inflexibility and rigid obstructiveness.

Money, money, money

Save for a rainy day and invest in your future. You don't know what's going to happen but expect the unexpected. Consider pensions early; even a small amount can grow big over time. Also, you can't take your hard-earned cash with you when you die; plan and spend sensibly. But do enjoy the fruits of your labours; you've earned it.

Interests

As you leap from one life stage to another, different hobbies, pastimes, sports, activities and interests will come into view. Age is not an inhibitor to learning something new. Give something different a go; you've got nothing to lose. If it doesn't work out, move on to the next one. You might even stumble across something which you're pretty good at and gives you a new lease of life.

Mental and physical health

Everyone gets knocks and bumps along the way, physical and mental. Being resilient helps you to manage and mitigate the effects. But appreciate that as you age you may experience increased limitations on body and mind. Accept this as normal and live within new parameters of capability.

Action Plan 28: Life Stage Reflection and Preparation

1. Consider the following life stages and where you exist at the present time.
2. Note any major conflict or trauma.
3. Record how you have or might work through these.
4. Write your major learning from each preceding life stage.
5. Assess potential threats or conflicts you see in the future.
6. Summarise all the opportunities you can sense for each future stage.

Age	Stage	Past conflict	Acceptance/ Resolution	Learning/ Insight	Future Threats	Future opportunities
0–1	Infancy					
1–3	Early childhood					
3–6	Pre-school					
6–13	Early school					
13–18	Puberty and adolescence					
18–21	Early adulthood					
21–30	Adulthood adaptation					
30–40	Family developments					
40–50	Career peak					
50–60	Clarity of life					
60–70	Taking it easier					
70–80	Managing capabilities					
80+	Coping with age					

29

Help: Asking for It and Finding It

Spotlight

Dictionary.com defines 'help' as *'to give or provide what is necessary to accomplish a task or satisfy a need; contribute strength or means to; render assistance to; cooperate effectively with; aid; assist'.*

We can't do everything on our own. As we grow through the stages of life, we learn new ways of doing things, of adapting to change and finding how to fit in and get on in life. Education and family nurturing can all help but at the end of the day, we're pretty much on our own. There's no life script or predestined path. And yet we can influence our present and future.

From time to time, we need answers, we need to know, we need inspiration and motivation, we need guidance and advice, we need nurturing, we need support in tough times and we need to share the joys in good times. We have many needs.

Most of us want to find our own answers or solutions and much of this does come from within; we know ourselves best and how we tick. But that doesn't always give us what we need.

Emotional and psychological conflict emerges when we get stuck in a rut, we feel trapped in a situation, we worry about something we can't sort out, we fear the unknown and can feel anxious about uncertainty or get depressed if we can't find a way out.

In most of these situations, asking the right person or going to the right place will offer us the answers to unlock us from this conflict. But we can sabotage this opportunity with stubbornness or ignorance. Our pride might prevent us from admitting we are stuck and don't know something. We might be anxious about appearing weak or vulnerable. Or our headstrong and rigid attitude might make us think only we can find the answer. But that's not always the case.

Sure, we can help ourselves and look for creative opportunities and solutions but we're not always in the place or zone to access this. Negative, stuck and repetitive thinking patterns can conspire against creative solutions. We can become fixated and obsessed, which can thwart the scope of opportunity.

We just need to ask for help. One of the best ways to ask for help is to help someone else. This might seem counterintuitive but it's our way of normalising, appreciating and accepting the value of what help is. If we can become more receptive to helping others, we learn how and when to ask for it. It makes it OK to ask for assistance.

Who you ask or where you go can be crucial to our developing the help habit. This resonates with the 'Dream Team' idea (see Chap. 19), which focused on identifying the most important, influential and appropriate people amongst family, friends, work and wider networks who you can tap into for different needs. This requires consideration about who you select for what.

If you needed help about a difficult relationship at work, you're going to get a different response from your partner, best friend, a work colleague, your manager and the Human Resources department. In this work example, assess what you need … do you need a formal resolution, work mediation, empathic understanding or just to vent your frustrations?

Top Tips

Needs assessment

So you need some assistance, but can you really drill down to the purpose and construct of that need? You may have both rational and emotive components which can fire off very different perspectives. Disentangle the matrix of variables to find clarity about what you really need.

Inspiration

Think of someone you admire who might be famous, in the media, a historical figure, a sporting legend, a respected elder or even a character from a book or TV show. What encouragement, inspiration or motivation would they give you if you were able to ask for their assistance?

Overload

If you are stuck in a rut, you may be overthinking and flooded by a sea of emotion. Siphon away these unhelpful and unproductive thoughts and emotions so you are left with a distilled clarity.

Projection

Consider the prospect that you may have an inaccurate understanding of your needs because you are projecting the wrong need on the situation. You might want help to find a new job but actually the best assistance might be to resolve a workplace problem in your current job.

Who are you?

Get to know how you tick; what gives you joy, what stresses you out? Understand the various family and work frameworks in which you live and how you interact within them. What shapes and drives your personality? You might feel an extrovert in some situations and more introverted in others. Why is this and how does this affect your capacity to ask for help?

Reluctance

If you are resistant to asking for help, ask yourself why this is the case. Is it stubbornness? Is it because you want to appear strong, not weak? Cross this hurdle and ask yourself what you can potentially gain from asking for help. Does it serve you best to remain stubborn and not get the help to move forward?

Rejection complex

An inhibitor to asking for help is that somehow the person we ask will reject us. Challenge this thought; will they really reject you? Even if they did, what's the worst that could result from this? And what's the probability of this happening?

Come in control

We like to have control over our lives and when we reach a point when we need help, we might feel that we're giving over this control to someone else. But you're actually doing the opposite by regaining control of a situation, which is essentially and actually not in your control anyway.

Dream team

Create a new contacts database, or an address book, which identifies key sources of help and assistance by topic. You might have a 'Career' section for those people who might influence your progression or offer mentoring or inspiration. You might also have a 'Moan' section to identify friends you can speak with when you just need to let off steam and vent frustrations.

Therapy

An independent coach, counsellor or therapist might also be worth considering. They should be able to give you impartiality and perspective to enable you to find your own solutions.

Action Plan 29: Helping Contacts List

Write into the boxes below the people who can help you in any of a range of potential future issues—add in a few of your own.

But also consider who YOU can help in similar situations—those you help might be more available to you when you need them. It can encourage you to connect with others, gives you a different perspective on your own problems and may enable you to feel that you can make a difference.

Issue	Who can help me?	Who can I help?
Anxiety and worries		
Apathy and de-motivation		
Low mood or depression		
Difficult relationships		
Work stress		
Career development		
Family challenges		
Health and fitness		
Legal		
Financial		
Housing and accommodation		
Consumer rights		
Electrician		
Plumber		
Construction or repairs		
Cleaning or gardening		
Social companionship		
Positive thinking and positivity		
Relaxation and peace		
Entertainment and fun		
Moan and vent stuff		
Sport, activity, hobby		

30

Being Childless or Child-Free

Spotlight

It doesn't matter what type of relationship you're in or not in, there can be strong urges to bring children into the world. Of course, there are also many people who exercise their right not to be a parent and not to have children, and they're perfectly happy with this choice (if it is a choice) or situation.

For many, though, it feels like there isn't the choice. Fertility issues, money problems and levels of affluence; career and job situation; locality and accommodation; family issues plus relationships and traumas from the past can all impact what happens and why, plus the choices or limitations on us.

It can be a highly emotive issue, with strong passions, opinions and judgements on both sides. 'Selfishness' always seems to come into the equation; is it selfish to want a child? Is it selfish not to want a child? What other people think has a huge influence on our own views, especially parents, family and friends. Parents have a complicated relationship here, because they can be tied up in their own needs or wants to be grandparents, or because they feel the nurturing they offered should be an automatically passed-down process. A sort of unquestioning, automatic, 'it's what you do' or 'what we did' idea. And it's why being childless or child-free remains a bit of a taboo subject.

Incidentally, we use the terms child-'free', as much as child-'less'. Childless seems to be used more commonly but has a negative, deficient connotation to it. Child-free has more positive choice energy. Both can apply and both resonate with the reality of the situation.

What is your reason, rationale or motivation for wanting a child? Some people do so without thinking or considering the responsibilities or obligations which will set them on a path potentially lasting for at least two decades.

Some believe that they need children in order to love, or be loved by, another person. Or they have attachment deficiencies and a child would fill this void. Or the relationship with a partner would work better if they were distracted with children. Or that the parents would relinquish some pressure and be more approving. Or that society would see them as more 'worthy and mature'. Or that it gives them 'respect' from others.

But children are not 'owned' by parents, they are the property of their world. We don't need to own children to delight in them and be a crucial part of their lives. The parent certainly is responsible for the child and amongst the massive shopping list of roles; nurtures, inspires, motivates, guides, disciplines, teaches, educates … cleans, washes, cooks and so on.

Child-free people often prevaricate over the losses of not having children, and, especially, of that sense of legacy, where they see children as the major legacy symbol which they don't have. But there are losses attributed to having children; to the loss of freedom, personal space, impact on relationships, to a diminished social life, to a loss of contact with friends, to a drain on finances and possibly career limitations.

Top Tips

Choice and control

What is important is not what you choose … but that you have choice.
Choice gives you control and sometimes you need to bring back control in whatever ways you can into a situation where you felt you had no control.

Partners

Allow for time to work through what's happening and don't assume there's mutual understanding or that one person is affected more than the other; it affects you both differently.

Changing view

It's quite normal that your feelings, thoughts, actions and choices may change and fluctuate. Give yourself (or yourselves) permission to change your mind and your views as part of 'processing'.

Success not failure

Consider the successes you can achieve without children, rather than failures attributed to not having children. There's always another side to how you can view things.

Mourn losses

It can feel unbearable and agonising to find you cannot have children when you wanted them. Find a way to take on this loss and mourn in a way which is right for you (both). It can take time, but do give it time, space and respect.

Rational versus emotional

You may oscillate between moments of rationality and having spontaneous emotional outbursts. You need logic and emotion, thoughts and feelings. Trust your instincts and intuition too, which is often your subconscious telling you something important.

Be all you can be

You (and your partner) are not defined by whether you have a child or not. You can do loads with your life. The possibilities really are endless. Only you can put the squeeze on your opportunities. Free yourself and let your body blossom; creatively with art, travel, friendships, hobbies, interests, work, volunteering, family or helping others.

Nurture others

Nurture the children of family and friends. They might all appreciate, and be inspired by, this.

Find peace

You might have very strong views and reasons to have children. But if you can't, you need to work through this reality, to accept and move on. This might conflict with core inner needs and values but your ultimate and most over-riding need is to survive. Survival comes from reconciliation.

Other options

If you cannot conceive yourself (yourselves), and are considering adoption, fostering, surrogacy, in vitro fertilisation (IVF) or any other option, do speak to as many people who have gone through this experience as possible. And make sure you get both sides. You need to hear the bad bits as well as the good bits.

Medical advice

Always seek a second opinion and don't assume that your doctor or consultant is correct all the time. They might be right, but another clinician may have a different perspective which might count.

Legacy

A legacy is not limited to having children but can be about an enduring relationship, inspiration and guidance for a niece or nephew, a book, blog, video produced or creative art which lives on.

Action Plan 30: What Is Your Legacy?

The Past: Tombstone Challenge

Imagine you dropped down dead today. What would you like your tombstone to say about you?

For example, *'She was a great listener?', 'He was a companion when you needed one?', 'She never said one word when 10 would do?', 'He was a true friend?', 'She inspired more than she knew?', 'His creativity knew no bounds', 'She made me laugh!'*

What would yours say?

_____

_____

_____

_____

The Present: Where Are You Now?

What change can you make today which will be remembered by others?

_____

_____

_____

_____

The Future: Where It Counts?

Who can you inspire, cherish, motivate, guide, enthral, captivate, enthuse, energise, educate, support and help?
It doesn't have to be a child. It could be a friend or acquaintance.
Start today and enjoy the journey …

_____

_____

_____

31

Pregnancy and Birth

Spotlight

This chapter is largely written for the mother who is, or potentially could be, pregnant. But as so much of a successful pregnancy involves the partner, family and friends, this may be relevant and helpful for them too.

Pregnancy can be an exciting or daunting experience depending on whether it was planned or not, the relationship with our partner, family and friends, our life circumstances and how prepared we are from a psychological point of view. What we choose to do next is a huge decision which will affect the rest of our lives. It will be further influenced by our work, home and financial situation, plans for the future, where we are in our own life cycle and the options, choices and consequences which might emerge from the decisions we might make.

Communicating how we are feeling to our partner or someone close to us is important to ensure that we don't start to feel isolated. The support, encouragement and insight from friends and family can be crucial too. Our feelings are also likely to change, sometimes frequently on any given day. This is normal and relates to the hormonal or emotional changes within our body.

How we respond and react to being pregnant can be significantly affected by previous experiences of childbirth (from our own and those of others), but each situation is different so it's helpful not to focus on anxieties about birth complications. Get advice and support from ante-natal classes, friends who have gone through the experience and other pregnant women.

We need to learn to trust our body and our instincts but also be aware that being tense or panicky can create problems not just during the pregnancy but also during the birth process. With understandably heightened anxiety, we need to find ways to be calm, chill out and relax (difficult that this might seem), maintaining interests, activities or hobbies. Mindfulness can help too.

There is a close interaction between body and mind, and pregnancy and birth is no exception. If we have physical problems, we need to get the facts, not by 'internetting' it, but by asking our doctor or midwife for reputable sources of information. We can gain assurances by utilising regular monitoring, checks and scans from healthcare professionals.

A good example of focusing on facts would be to write out and construct a birth plan. This is a proactive way to involve someone close to us and to think through what we would like to happen from an ideal point of view. The process also starts to prepare us for the different scenarios that may occur during the birth and helps us work through the options available. Whilst a birth plan allows some structure and focus, they don't always turn out as expected. We'll always need to expect the unexpected.

Top Tips

Listen to your feelings

Finding out you are pregnant and then thinking about the birth process can produce many strong feelings of anxiety. You may be saying to yourself 'how will I cope?', 'that's the end of my freedom', 'I'm worried about whether I can be a good mother/father', 'I can't cope with the pain that will happen and I hate needles'. These anxieties are normal and it is likely you will experience them. These thoughts will pass and you will be able to work through them. Give yourself time, identify who can offer a listening ear and speak with them.

Doubts

If you have doubts about having the baby, speak to your partner about how you are feeling as a joint decision is helpful and this can enable you to work through what is going to be best for all concerned. Avoid rushing into any decisions and do seek counsel from medical healthcare professionals as well as those experienced in providing psychological support. Consider seeing a therapist to explore your thoughts and feelings and to work through your decision. There are a lot of organisations available to help. Reaching out to them can reduce feelings of confusion and isolation.

Work stuff

Especially if this is your first baby decide whether to work or how much to work. Your employer has a Duty of Care towards you when pregnant and it is useful to know your rights. Get advice from people at work, such as Occupational Health or Human Resources, who can guide you through the process. This may include having breaks, time off to attend appointments, maternity and paternity pay after birth, leave (pre- and post-birth) and sickness absence. If in doubt, seek advice from your Citizens Advice Bureau, Employee Assistance Programme or your Union.

Communication at work

Keep your employer informed of your situation and communicate what helps and what is not helping regarding adjustments to your work. Work colleagues may need to cover some of your work so anticipate that some may react negatively. However, the majority will usually be pleased for you and look forward to hearing progress.

Relaxation

Relaxation is not the first word that comes into mind when thinking about pregnancy and giving birth. But caring for your body is important, not just in terms of what you eat and drink but also the rest you achieve, such as, listening to music, engaging in a relaxing pastime or hobby, having a bath, watching TV, using mindfulness or practising yoga. There may be support and exercise groups available in your locality. Involve your partner where this helps relax you.

Keep active

As your body starts to change, it can be tempting to avoid exercise. Keeping active is still as important as ever and undertaking light exercise will help you keep toned and supple. Seek advice if you have any complications or when light exercise starts to cause pain.

Physical and psychological

A host of 'normal' reactions might occur, such as noticing your ligaments soften, back pain, nausea, heartburn and vomiting. You might also find that your moods become more erratic and exaggerated. If in doubt, check it out with your doctor or midwife.

Action Plan 31: Pregnancy Preparation Plan

You might not think about pregnancy until you are pregnant and then when you are, you'll have so many thoughts swirling round in your head that you might not know where to begin!

A good place to start is to write a checklist and tick off the points as you work through them.

Pretty much every situation is unique, so consider the big picture and add to the checklist with points to consider that fit you and your circumstances.

✓

- ☐ Know how pregnancy will change your body.
- ☐ Stop smoking and drinking alcohol.
- ☐ Learn what relaxes you.
- ☐ Know the steps of seeing your doctor, nurse and midwife as well as the timings of having ultrasounds and scans.
- ☐ Prepare for possible disruptions such as morning sickness, headaches and tiredness.
- ☐ Decide when to stop working.
- ☐ Learn about the process of having a baby in hospital or at home including pain relief during the labour process.

- Prepare a birth plan—what will happen how, where, when and with whom?
- Get advice on the essentials of having a baby such as nappies, bottle/breastfeeding, washing your baby and the equipment you need such as a cot and pram.
- Communicate how you are feeling to those close to you during all the above as you are going to need the support.
- Celebrate the new arrival!
- Watch out for post-natal depression or 'baby blues' and speak to your midwife or doctor if you start to feel low.
- Attend both ante-natal and post-natal classes, as these will provide much needed information, insight and support, as well as giving you potential new friends.

32

Parenting Pre-teens

Spotlight

This chapter covers the child's journey from being a toddler, through nursery and primary school in readiness to becoming young adults.

The age span is wide and the tasks of being a parent can change quite significantly from when our child learns how to walk, speaks and becomes toilet-trained, through the tantrum years and into the world of socialising with other children and learning how to behave at school. Although we are addressing parents, the principles apply to any caregiver involved in supporting the child, such as a guardian, relative, grandparent or a significant other.

Being a parent is often described as a thankless task. It has many challenges and we can often feel overwhelmed and unprepared for what happens, especially if our child becomes ill or has an accident. A child's behaviours can also cause problems and it can be difficult to know how strict to be; very strict and authoritarian or taking a more relaxed carefree approach.

The first preoccupation often involves thoughts on being a 'good enough' parent. Being a parent is not easy and we all make mistakes including saying and doing the wrong things. It is a steep learning curve and there's often no obvious right or wrong way to do things. We learn along the way. Even if there was a complete 'How to be a Parent' encyclopaedia out there, things change all the time and we find we need to adapt and make instinctive and snap decisions in the moment. No book can help us in these situations. But bit by bit, we do learn what works and what doesn't.

Perfection is not achievable but being 'good enough' is about always being open to learning from any mistakes, focusing on loving our child by giving them affection and encouragement, setting them boundaries but also knowing that, in turn and in time, we will probably need physical and emotional support ourselves during these early years.

Top Tips

Plan fun activities

Children respond to play. Getting down to their level during play allows for meaningful communication. With a toddler sit or kneel down and ensure you have focused eye contact. Use your facial and verbal expressions to communicate your emotions. With older children, pick games that they enjoy. And don't try to win them!

Keepsafe

Create a diary or 'keepsafe' book of your child's development as this will be a wonderful way of capturing your memories of them.

Bedtime

Develop clear routines at bed times, be consistent and keep the environment calm. Reading a story is a connecting way to bond with your child and reassures them by your voice which helps them get ready for sleep. Avoid boisterous or energetic games and be aware of the effect of your voice; try to speak with soft calm tones rather than a loud, excited alternative. Ditch the TV, mobile phones and tablet devices.

Playtime

Support your child in their friendships, set up 'play dates' with school friends and talk to your child about the games they enjoy playing. The best games can involve dressing up, role-playing or encouraging them to engage in an imaginary world. Avoid an over-reliance on computer games as these can over-stimulate and discourage socialisation. Motivate your children to burn off excess energy with outdoor pursuits, hobbies, interests and sports.

Peer conflict

Help your child normalise negotiation with their friends, especially if there is a conflict or issues of jealousy. Spot signs of conflict early on, so these can quickly be identified, discussed and resolved.

Disappointment

Your child needs to learn how to deal with disappointment, whether with their friendships, not winning in sports or not getting what they want when they want it. Being a good role model will help them learn. You may need to adapt and change how to do things too, including how YOU deal with disappointment.

Choosing the battles

If you try to win all the battles you will exasperate your child and exhaust yourself so work out which battles to win. Whatever you decide, be consistent and be resolute. Highlight the consequences for your child if they 'cross the line' and always be prepared to follow through, highlighting the consequences.

The rules

Both parents need to determine and play by the same set of rules otherwise the child will get mixed and confused messages. Unclear, ambiguous or different rules will encourage the child to manipulate one parent against the other. Involve wider family and other caregivers too.

The power of encouragement and praise

Often relationship problems between a parent and their child are caused by a downward cycle of discouragement where the parent is negative and often criticises what the child is doing. The child may respond by continuing to be 'naughty' as this is their way of getting your attention. This cycle needs to be broken with the positive power of praise. Find something that your child does right, be specific with your praise and give them attention. The idea is to eliminate the negative behaviours by trying to ignore them.

Our own parents

We have all been parented in some way and this experience shapes our way of parenting children. Some of us may have had traumatic and abusive experiences. We may react by consciously parenting in a totally different way than our parents. But we may not be that aware of how we have been influenced. Examples include behaviour discipline, 'rules' or attitudes to bedtime. Reflect and acknowledge that your own approach is influenced by your parents. Avoid disputing with your parents whose approach is best or 'right'. Agree a new strategy where both parties have an input and the end result is a more creative and positive outcome. Set boundaries with your own parents as you are the person responsible for your children. But don't avoid or ignore them. Your parents may be a key to your child's learning, development and support, and offer stability and reassurance.

Action Plan 32: Hopes for Your Child

List the hopes you have for your child, that is to become a confident person, learn the value of creativity, honesty, trust, transparency, enjoy nature and the outdoors, play music, dance and so on.

_____

_____

_____

Which are the most important 'hopes' and why? Are they your vicarious hopes, that is things you didn't have or get (this isn't necessarily good or bad, as long as you are aware of the motives)?

1. _____

2. _____

3. _____

For these three hopes, what do you need to do to set these in motion?

1. _____
2. _____
3. _____

What support do you need from others and who are these people?

_____

_____

_____

Finally, to help you to help your child, you need some time and space for YOU? How will you find yours and what will you do?

_____

_____

_____

33

Parenting Teenagers

Spotlight

The development from puberty through to growing up into an adult brings complicated challenges, including huge anxieties about change, especially starting a new school. But it brings challenges for the parent too, as we adapt to these changes and start to transition from a relationship of dependence into independence.

With teenage years come hormones, a big appetite and lots of emotional ups and downs. As parents we also share in the roller coaster of emotions including, but not limited to, periods of confusion, fear, anxiety and feeling overwhelmed. The teenage years mark an important period of change into adulthood.

Our teenager may feel unlovable during this transition, especially if they are more focused on going out, seeing their friends and being ferried around by us. However, underneath they still need to know they are loved. And we still need to know that some of their 'unlovable' behaviours will pass. If we shape and communicate the values we want them to integrate, these will eventually take hold.

Given all the changes, it can be an exhausting time for the teenager. Keeping our home environment as supportive as possible is going to be important to see them through to the other side. Our young adult will seek to challenge us in many different ways and it can be tempting to react to them. But it will offer affirmation and reassurance to keep connected to them and to avoid unnecessary conflict over things that aren't really that important.

We need to identify what is a 'red line' or important issue and hold strong to that but also have the humility to admit when we have overreacted or got it wrong and are prepared to negotiate with them. They will respect us much more for this.

It can be a painful reality to think that the child we brought into the world is going to grow up and leave us one day, yet this is reality and we need to be confident in knowing that the foundations we built in them will help them in their lives. Holding on to our children psychologically and preventing them developing into adults out of fear will probably mean that they will, at some point, want to separate from us anyway. It is better to gradually give them freedom, encouragement and independence and to acknowledge that this means they are going to be less dependent on us rather than holding them back or trying to control them.

There is nothing quite like hearing how we have been a positive role model. Being a parent is an amazing opportunity to influence our children. We can share our experiences as well as our mistakes. Work hard to find ways to build up our relationship with them, take an interest in what they are doing and communicate our values with them.

Top Tips

Stay in relationship

Your young adult needs your relationship, perhaps even more so than when they were younger. Even if they appear on the surface to want the opposite, use all the daily living tasks to reach out and connect with them, such as when driving them to an event or shopping with them.

Decisions, decisions

Empower your teenager so that they feel they can make decisions without you but also help them understand the consequences of different actions. Yes, you want them to make good decisions, but if they aren't given the opportunity to do this they won't learn. You want to trust that your child will learn from decisions they make, whether these are the right decisions or not.

Trust

Trusting your young adult is crucial, so avoid prying too much into exactly what they are doing with their friends, however inquisitive you are. As a teenager their peer group is really important and they may seem like they are ignoring all your advice. This is normal but believe in the values you have taught them to help shape them and the decisions they make. Trust remains two-way.

Celebrate

The pressures on your children can be immense during the teenage years, including examinations, social media 'likes', friendship issues, fitting in, dealing with disappointment and so on. As the parent, you have an important role to celebrate them; to celebrate their unique personality, their skills and interests, their sense of humour, evolving passions and beliefs, and their developing sense of perspective on the world about them. Look for every opportunity to inspire, motivate and encourage them.

Find an exit

It can be tempting to labour a lesson learnt with 'I told you so'. However, it is more powerful, and a better learning tool, to support them even when they have made a wrong choice and to allow them to acknowledge this with you. If they are cornered by you, it can create a 'lose–lose' situation. Instead, always give them an exit. 'I told you so' isn't going to help anyone.

Action Plan 33: Shared Activity Strategy

List the top five activities you currently share with your young adult:

1. _____

2. _____

3. _____

4. _____

5. _____

Identify how much you are really 'available' to them during these activities, that is, physically, emotionally and engagement-wise. Rate each activity from a scale of 1–10 where '1' is not available and '10' is totally involved with them during the activity. How can you increase your availability?

Activity	Availability Score 1–10

If you are not enjoying your involvement with a particular activity, your young adult will pick up this apathy and lack of enthusiasm. Using the same rating scale, 1–10, rate how much you and your teenager enjoy the activities. Focus on the ones with the highest scores, but get variety too.

Activity	Your enjoyment 1–10	Their enjoyment 1–10

What distractions are getting in the way for you to be more psychologically and physically involved with, or available to, your young adult? (We suspect a mobile phone might be on this list!)

1. _____
2. _____
3. _____
4. _____
5. _____

What can you change or propose to do differently from here on?

1. _____
2. _____
3. _____

34

When Children Leave Home

Spotlight

For those who have children, it can seem like it takes a lifetime (theirs and yours) for them to grow up. Then all of a sudden they are no longer the toddlers, little people, the teenagers they once were. They have become full-fledged adults. 'Empty Nest Syndrome' is the phrase used to describe when a child leaves home, or flees the nest, and the feelings of loss and abandonment which can be felt by the parent.

Children come into this world totally dependent on the parent and yet from the point of birth the slow, gradual process of detachment and independence takes place. The children are finding their voice, their place in the world, their identity and personality, and in order for them to run with this, we have to release them, we have to give them up as ours. They are not ours, they are theirs.

Our job is to raise them to be happy, confident and independent adults, but we do have to let them go and this can raise huge attachment issues for both sides. The young adult will be losing a degree of safety and security, the parent will be losing the roles and responsibility of providing that safety and security.

They've moved on, excited and enthusiastic about the challenges and opportunities in front of them, and whilst we might vicariously share that, we are also left feeling bereft. A third, maybe half our lives have been dedicated to or caught up in being their parent, and now that role has changed. We'll always be their parent, that won't change. But in a way, everything else has changed. The relationship has changed.

It's not the same without them. You now hear the deafening noise of silence. You miss their messy rooms, their crumbs on the kitchen table, the dirty clothes strewn across their bedroom floor, the din of bizarre pop music, some of their annoying friends, and pacing around in the small hours when they didn't come back when they said they would. You'd have that all back in a flash.

If you live with your partner and this is your last child to 'flee the nest', you will have the new pressure of life going back to the two of you again. There may be feelings of loneliness.

But life changes and any loss feels painful; like bereavement (see Chap. 27). And it'll take time to adjust and find a new way of being. Things have changed and they will be different. But it can also be about embracing the change, moving with it and shaping it in a way that helps everyone. The new way. But first you have to mourn the loss.

Of course, there will be some parents who will escape Empty Nest Syndrome because they can't wait for their children to leave home. Levels of affluence, education, debt, property prices, opportunity and relationships may mean children stay at home into their 20s and 30s, maybe longer. Every situation is different; it might be a win-win for all concerned… or a total nightmare. It also depends on how you get on with your kids… and your partner.

Top Tips

Accept the change

The child has left, whether through choice or not, for a job, education, relationship, travel or opportunities. The first stage is accepting this reality. Accept they have gone. It can be tough.

Still the parent

You will always be the parent however far away they are or what little contact you might have. Nothing changes that or the memories which you can cherish.

Feel the feelings

Acknowledge the loss and the different feelings you experience. Speak to your partner, friend, colleague or therapist or coach about this; get it off your chest. If you feel sad and bereft, especially if you hold regrets about the way in which your child has left home (maybe following an argument or disagreement) it's important for you to express how you feel. If you feel angry and frustrated, find a way to release this, so it doesn't churn you up and dig away inside you.

Avoid comparisons

It can be easy to fall into comparing what it was like when you were young; 'I was working in a local shop when I was 14' might have been true for you, but whilst legislation has undoubtedly changed, so have the opportunities. Appreciate the perspective of your child not yours.

New relationship

Whilst still the parent, you have an opportunity to forge a new style of relationship with the child. What about seeing yourself as more of a mentor or coach, where you offer timely adult guidance? You don't make the rules anymore, at least not in the same way as before.

Adult to adult

The big challenge for both parent and child is the notion, and novelty, of both learning to develop a relationship where you engage at the adult-to-adult level, with a more equal power-balance and power-sharing. As the parent, you always had authority over the child. Now it's different. It can be difficult for both to adapt; for the child to take the responsibility and for the parent to give it.

New era

Your role has changed, and so do the opportunities—consider new plans, initiatives, hobbies, pastimes, pursuits, interests and so on. You may have time on your hands to do the things you never felt you had the time for. Go for it. The time is yours.

Partnerships and relationships

Relationships change when children leave. Suddenly you might have a very different relationship with your partner or other family members, for the better or the worst. Some couples find that they stayed together 'for the children' and that now they have gone, so has any inclination to stay with the partner. But don't do anything too rash. Make the time to work together and stay together.

Keep in touch

Negotiate how you keep in touch, when, why and how. Your choices will determine whether you have successfully allowed your child to 'be free' or whether you still control the shots. Can you occasionally share new sports or activities with them? Enjoy meeting their friends.

Action Plan 34: 'Have I Got Needs for You' Model

As you negotiate and adjust the 'letting go', you're still allowed contact, you can still see them, you can still phone or message them. The challenge is working out between you what is 'appropriate' contact and communication between you which is in both your interests. It's not necessarily that meeting your needs is right or wrong, but you have to consider whether you are doing things for the right reasons, motivations and outcomes.

ACTION	MY NEEDS OR THEIRS?
Examples:	
Phone to check they are OK each evening	*More my needs*
Check monthly they have enough money	*Their needs*
Offer advice about money management	*Their needs*
Give them money if they come to see me	*Mutual needs*
Tell them I can do their washing	*Bit of both—but healthy?*
Insisting I meet their new partner	*More my needs*

Consider your actions and determine whose needs these meet; yours or theirs.

ACTION	MY NEEDS OR THEIRS?
_____	_____
_____	_____
_____	_____
_____	_____
_____	_____
_____	_____

Get feedback on how they are adjusting to the new dynamics and negotiate new ways of interacting.

_____

_____

_____

35

Embracing a Mid-life Crisis

Spotlight

The term 'mid-life crisis' can be a bit misleading. You're unlikely to wake up one morning and suddenly find yourself in the throes of such a crisis. It's more likely to be a dawning realisation, emerging over a period of time. Even the 'mid-life' bit. When is mid-life these days; when you are in your 30s, 40s, 50s or 60s? It's about our perception of age. How young do we feel? By referring to a 'mid-life crisis' we feed a potential inevitability that we will all experience such a thing, when many people will not.

Life is about a series of events, experiences, stages and cycles; some amazing, some tragic and the majority somewhere in between. Being resilient is about embracing our collection of experiences and learning to adapt and run with the consequences, so that we become architects of our lives, and have the power and scope to shape our destiny, whatever that might be.

A 'mid-life crisis' can best be described by the feelings which may emerge. We may feel dissatisfied by things from our past, or frustrated by inertia and apathy in the present, or angst that time is running out for future life ambitions. It can be triggered by life events, such as children leaving home or getting married or divorced, of changing job or of shifts in our relationships. It can also become evident by our behaviours and things we do and maybe rash things. We might feel a compulsion to go on adventurous travels or buy some snazzy sports car to recoup that inner youth.

Everything within this links back to our ageing process, reflecting on and perhaps yearning for our youth. And that's why some people choose to end a relationship and seek someone younger, in an attempt to make themselves feel younger. But we can't fight ageing and that's the angst behind mid-life crisis. We spend so much time, effort and money wanting to appear younger and youthful… there comes a time when the reality hits us.

As we age, more people around us pass away. And we start to think of our own life and death. Thinking about one's mortality raises powerful and fundamental issues about ourselves and our place in the world. We start to realise that the clock is ticking and time is running out.

In our teens and twenties, we didn't really think of middle or old age. We were too busy trying to work out life as a youngster, thinking about a career path, maybe searching for a partner and possibly experimenting with lots of stuff and having fun in the process. We didn't need to be too serious or settle down or be too mature. We had faith then that we would stumble across our pot of gold, in terms of career, affluence, relationships and family and so on. But before you know it, we're on that career conveyor-belt, relationships, homes and bang. We're suddenly in our 30s, 40s, 50s, 60s and maybe that pot of gold hasn't materialised after all.

Hopes and dreams may remain largely unfulfilled.

Top Tips

Who ARE you?

Write down who and what you are; your identity and personality. Where have you come from, what have you achieved, how would others describe you? Do you recognise this person?

Mortality

What does thinking about your own death bring up for you? If it freaks you out, ask why? Your answers may help you understand what you are feeling and, importantly, some of the choices you may need to make for the future as denial and fear actually limits your choices.

Zig-zag life path

There's no such thing as a life-script, predefined at birth, even if you are a member of some royal dynasty. Stuff happens, things change. We have to go with the flow, roll with the punches and end up where we end up. Fate or destiny weaves its own complex tartan tapestry.

Accept the past

Sadness, guilt and regret about the past needs to be let go, somehow. You can't change what's happened (or not happened) but you can change whether you feel trapped by your past and how you feel about it today. How can you acknowledge the past, appreciate the impact on you, but then maybe compartmentalise, close the door and move on? You control how you deal with your past, it doesn't control or define you.

Appreciate maturity

You are bound to have memories which you wince about, concerning your naivety of youth, things you said and did which make you blush with embarrassment or squirm in awkwardness. Enjoy feeling smug about how older, mature and wiser you are now!

Restlessness

If you are feeling frustrated, angst or restless, what's this about? What is this saying to you? If you feel hopeless and meaningless, then maybe you need some hope and meaning. Who can help you in this quest?

Menopause

Men and women both experience hormonal, physiological and chemical changes in the body as we age, which can set off a series of responses. The changes are different for everyone with the most well known being the menopause. Have a conversation with your doctor or there may be support groups in your locality.

Manage limitations

A sign of ageing is our body refusing to do what it could when younger. Rather than what you can't do now, what are all the things that you can do, including things you've never done before?

Time for change

Start making some plans. Fancy spending more time with your family (or less)? Or working part-time or volunteering? What's your financial situation and what choices does this give you? Or what hobbies or interests have you always wanted to try?

Action Plan 35: Mid-life Choices and Consequences Model

Choice: What would rejuvenate your body, mind or spirit or give you added purpose, meaning, fulfilment and nourishment?

Consequence: What would be the consequences of this, positive or negative?

Conclusion: So is this a YES or a NO?

CHOICE	CONSEQUENCES	CONCLUSION
Examples:		
Take up snowboarding	*Exciting new skill but I have an old hip problem*	NO
Beekeeping	*I enjoy nature and love honey*	YES
Volunteer	*Gives back to community and could be sociable*	YES
Write your own …		
1. _____	_____	___
2. _____	_____	___
3. _____	_____	___
4. _____	_____	___
5. _____	_____	___
6. _____	_____	___
7. _____	_____	___
8. _____	_____	___
9. _____	_____	___
10. _____	_____	___

Take your YES options and go for it!

36

Addictions

Spotlight

We are all potentially addicted to something, whether it is to social media, food, exercise, watching the news or more harmful behaviours such as smoking, gambling, alcohol or recreational drugs.

Whatever the addiction may be, we are likely to feel limited control over the behaviours and may have developed a physical or psychological dependency. This means that without a 'fix' of the particular behaviour we may start to feel a strong 'need' or, in more serious cases, struggle to cope with daily life. In some cases the dependency may be so strong that we feel unable to function.

Being addicted to a substance or activity usually means that we are dependent on it and that the more we engage with it the greater the tolerance to it, which means that we need more to achieve the same result. Addiction fits on a physical and psychological continuum, meaning that some are more physical, others psychological and the rest a mix of the two.

We could be 'addicts' without any apparent problems. But the insidious nature of addiction is that we're not aware it is causing us problems until the problems burst out, potentially impacting negatively our mental health and putting a strain on our relationships. Relationships are usually the first to suffer in most addictions.

The dilemma with any addiction is our failure to acknowledge that we have a problem with it. This is called denial and it can mean that only when we are at 'rock bottom' will we accept that the addiction needs to be addressed. Unfortunately, this often happens after a lot of damage has been caused and we may have lost our sense of ourselves and alienated those close to us.

With many abstinence-focused addiction recovery associations, such as the worldwide Alcoholics Anonymous, the first important step before any other and above all else is to accept, acknowledge and admit that we have a problem. We may feel on our own, but there are many different organisations available that can provide treatment, support and advice for people with addictions. However, for serious addictions it is always important to consult your doctor.

Top Tips

Social drinking

Probably the most common and destructive addiction, because of its widespread availability, alcohol is a huge part of social activity. Young people are pulled into the society norm of drinking and can feel isolated if not conforming to the apparent 'norm' of drinking. Buck the trend and spend a night out with your friends consuming non-alcoholic drinks instead. Some people alternate a soft drink and an alcoholic drink. Others choose something that looks like an alcoholic drink. Look around you at the end of the evening to see if you like the behaviours being exhibited around you. You can still have a laugh and be the life and soul of the party without drinking alcohol. Try it.

Binge-drinking

Many people, particularly in the UK, engage in a quest, usually at weekends, to pretty much drink as much as they can until they fall over. It's often about getting into a mind-altering wipe-out, where the drinker is seeking to escape or forget their reality. Your wallet and hangover will tell you if this applies to you. Ask yourself what's wrong with your life and you'll probably come up with a pretty accurate diagnosis, which will help you identify what you need to do to effect change. Fill your life with activities, interests and pursuits which better define you, nurture you and nourish you.

Workaholic

Many people are addicted to work to the extent that it preoccupies their whole life. Of course, work does take up a large and important part of our normal working day, but it is how we balance this. If you lost your job tomorrow, how would you cope? How can you create a better work–life balance? (see Chap. 42).

Gambling—the hidden addiction

Gambling is often referred to as the 'hidden addiction', as there are few outward signs until there are serious financial, relationship and psychological consequences. Pay your bills before you gamble and hang around with people who don't gamble. Regard gambling as not a way to make money, rather it's part of the 'entertainment' industry that makes money from you. Consider why you 'need' to gamble. What's the pay off? Is the risk worth it? What local support groups are available?

Smoking

Everyone knows that smoking is physically harmful. If you continue to smoke tobacco, it may kill you. From the first day you stop you will feel better, physically. You'll feel something different every day, until the benefits will out-win any urge to smoke again. Some people transition away from tobacco with nicotine patches or gum, others transfer to e-cigarettes or vaping, others find no substitutes are necessary. There are smoking cessation support groups and doctors and Pharmacies may offer options too. Everyone's different. You choose what works for you.

Internet

The internet has transformed life and is probably the greatest invention since the steam engine. Yet it is the source of a new addiction, particularly social media, where we may have a Fear Of Missing Out or FOMO. Everyone presents an elevated and enhanced view of themselves on social media, having the most amazing fun. But it's not real. It's edited highlights. Limit your social media time to a set, short period. Don't tune in at other times and switch off alerts on your mobile devices. Go and do all the things that others pretend they're doing.

Porn addiction

Online pornography is the 'silent' addiction because it's usually done alone and people don't talk about it, yet it's an increasingly pervasive addiction. You'll know if this applies to you. If it does, ditch the fantasy world and re-engage with the real world. Focus on relationships which really matter. Understand your sexual drives and motivations. If they're consensual and not harmful, find effective ways to realise them. Seek professional help if you're having difficulties, either via your doctor or a sex therapist.

Shopping addiction

The bright lights and funky music of shops mimic the fruit machines in betting shops. It titillates our senses. Some people need to buy things (for themselves or others) to make them feel good about themselves, but it can leave them skint or with feelings of shame. Alternatively, some people get a buzz from spotting a bargain or amazing find in charity shops or auction houses. Or making things themselves as part of a hobby. Or visiting a gallery, cinema or coffee house instead of a shop. Or enjoying what they have already.

Choose Life

The choices of social activities often determine whether they encroach on to a potentially addictive behaviour. If you want to stop drinking alcohol, don't go to bars. If you have a problem with gambling, avoid betting shops. If you have internet addiction, get off the computer. Do something else. Choose something different which enriches you. Choose life.

Choose abstinence

Before stopping any harmful addiction, particularly alcohol and recreational drugs, speak to your doctor, as a sudden halt can have unintended withdrawal consequences. Once you have done this, try stopping. What will help you most is to map out the benefits or how much better you feel on a daily basis afterwards. Use a diary to chart each and every benefit. Read this back routinely.

Positive addictions

Think about how more positive addictions can sometimes be of use, such as exercise, keeping the house tidy or creating a nature-friendly garden. However, keep this in balance and moderate this with aspects of your life where you are not addicted to something. Everything in moderation. Monitor whether you are replacing one harmful addiction with another.

Ask for help

An addiction can be excruciatingly difficult to shift, manage and eradicate. Some of us can do it on our own, maybe with the advice of our doctor. But for most of us, we need support, assistance and the patience of those around us. Kicking an addiction is often regarded as a team effort. Who can you identify as your Dream Team of Addiction-Kickers?

Action Plan 36: Do I Have an Addiction?

Consider the following statements and whether they apply to you. If they do, you may have an addiction that needs attention or managing.

✓

- ☐ You start to have memory lapses in relation to what you have been doing.
- ☐ Someone has suggested to you that you have an addiction problem, or ask someone close to you if they think you have a problem.
- ☐ You start to tell lies in relation to an addiction or hide your actions from others.

- ☐ You feel your addiction has led you into debt or triggered other relationship or work problems.
- ☐ You start to exhibit risky behaviours.
- ☐ You start to rely on the addiction as a form of escapism.
- ☐ You begin to take time off work due to your addiction.
- ☐ You feel you cannot cope without your 'crutch'.
- ☐ You become frustrated, angry, anxious or aggressive if you cannot have your 'crutch'.

Only you can accept whether you have an addiction, and if so, whether you intend to do something about it.

37

Being Single

Spotlight

There's this weird perception that you can only be happy if you are in a relationship. The reality is that you need to be happy in yourself BEFORE you can have a relationship. But society gets this wrong, as if 'being in a relationship' is the solution. It can actually mask or make the problem worse. You can't really love someone else and be with another, if you haven't learnt to love and be with yourself. You are 50% of any relationship. If you have problems going into a relationship how is a relationship going to sort it out?

Every one of us starts in this world as a single person. Sure we might be somewhat dependant on our parents or carers but we're still a single, unique individual. Pressures do start to emerge as we form relationships, there's always someone asking 'so do you have a boy/girl-friend yet?'. What's it to them if we do or do not? In fact, what's it to us if we do or do not? So what?

We can have very close relationships with people and remain single. Conversely, we can be in a relationship with someone and have no intimacy or sense of relationship. It's how we connect to others and build up trust through intimacy and communication.

We often get this drive that we MUST be in a relationship; that society will judge us as being inadequate, our friends will see us as deficient or our family will believe we have some sexuality issue. Lots of judgements which have nothing to do with other people. Many people have an opinion on a topic that's none of their business! And especially if it's not about them.

There's not just pressure to be in a relationship, but the stage before we're even in a relationship; dating. Somehow we need to be seen to be active and engaged in 'getting out there' and meeting potential mates. But dating can put the fear of death into so many people. There are so many types of online dating websites nowadays, ways of meeting people and hooking up, thanks to a web profile and some chatty copy. But it's also become quite impersonal too.

A couple of generations ago, men and women went to dances en masse, and you'd partner up to dance and if you got on, then great, but it was an activity-based process. A generation ago it was the discos, raves and parties; again, concerned with the music and relating to each other. But now it's so much more focused on 'dating', especially 'online dating'—the need to find someone attractive via an online profile which probably is nothing like reality and is totally focused on looks and the 'chat'. It's a bit of a minefield.

Be careful out there.

Top Tips

Try something new

Leap out of your comfort zone and be adventurous. Being single often makes us retreat from opportunities when we actually have fewer restraints from others to limit our potential. Be daring, be brave, be ambitious, be you. Enjoy being single.

Trust your instinct

Your intuition is a powerful force for good. It's like an unconscious awareness which you can embrace and enjoy as your ally and support.

Who are you?

Love yourself. Get to know and understand how you tick and what makes you who you are. How would others describe you and how different is this to your perception of you? Why the difference?

Meet people unconditionally

Once you have your 'partner radar' switched on, you lose spontaneity and impulsiveness. Ask people questions and you come across as interesting, because you're showing interest in others. Your future mate is probably going to be attracted to you when you are just being natural and not trying too hard.

Learn something new

Study, read up or educate yourself about something you have an interest in. Rejuvenate an interest from something in school that fired your enthusiasm but you have lost touch with since.

Develop self-awareness

Understand one new thing about yourself every day. Ponder on your emotional reservoir—why do you feel the way you do in response to triggers? What stresses, calms or relaxes you?

Cleanse the past

Identify the emotional baggage from past relationships and find ways to ditch what pulls you down.

Do things alone

You need to enjoy being with yourself without pressure to BE with someone. Go for a walk, a swim, to the movies, to the library, browse second hand shops, visit a gallery or museum, pop into an arts studio, go to a concert, watch a great film … the list is endless.

You choose

Being single means you don't have to compromise or negotiate with anyone else. You decide what you do, when you do it. You're in control of you. You're the boss. Enjoy the freedom.

Friend introductions

If you have friends you trust, the chances are they will have friends they trust. Ask to be introduced to your friends' friends and boost your friendship network. Nurture friendships which are good for you and ditch the ones which are not. Life's too short.

Help out

Giving something back makes you feel good. Volunteer with a charity, help out at a food bank, muck in at a farm, chip in with an elderly group, sort out at a book shop or do some conservation work.

Dating tips

If you are ready to date, get testimonials from friends who have used dating websites; the good and the bad. Tell a friend if you're meeting someone for a date, ask them to call you at a set time, don't drink too much, keep the first date short, you can both meet up again if it works out. Take things easy, you have plenty of time and plenty of other options. You just haven't found him/her yet.

Action Plan 37: 'Getting to Know You' Audit

Answer the following questions. If you don't have an answer, find one. Not only will you begin to appreciate yourself more (i.e. there's a lot about you), but you'll also increase self-confidence.

1. What's your best physical feature?

   _____

2. What do your friends like about you most?

   _____

3. How do you express your creativity?

   _____

4. What art or music gives you depth?

_____

5. What moves you most emotionally?

_____

6. What makes you laugh out loud on your own?

_____

7. Who most inspires you and why?

_____

8. What gives you an inner peace or calmness?

_____

9. What did you last do to help someone else?

_____

10. Identify the benefits of being single.

_____

11. How do you energise yourself?

_____

12. What sport or exercise do you enjoy most?

_____

13. Where would you like to travel to and why?

_____

14. What new interest or hobby could you start?

_____

15. What could you make as a present for someone?

_____

16. How do you tap into your spirituality?

_____

17. What do you love most about your family?

_____

18. How do you treat or pamper yourself?

_____

19. What's a knock-out recipe or meal you can make?

_____

20. What can you do to change your life for the better (being single)?

_____

38

Personal Wellness Toolkit

Spotlight

Being 'well' involves the physical, mental, emotional, spiritual and psychological. Before any of us make changes to our lifestyle, we need to assess what is within our healthy capabilities, so may require us to check with a doctor what is suitable. It can be fruitful to ask for a mini-check-up of our vital statistics, such as blood pressure, body mass index (weight to height ratio) and general fitness level. Most health practices have facilities to measure and monitor us.

Regular exercise will contribute to helping us feel more naturally tired at the end of the day and allow us to get a good sleep. But sleep can be fickle and if we're not getting the amount of sleep that we need it can have a significant impact on our mood and concentration. A routine and disciplined sleep regime might be required.

Assuming we sleep well, we'll awake at breakfast time, which may trigger the start of the nutritional nourishment we'll take in over the day. A healthy diet is one that sustains us for the demands of the day and limits the excessive 'bad' foods which can tire us and contribute to weight gain and apathy. A healthy diet can also help to protect us from medical conditions such as diabetes.

Then we'll work at something; whether this is school work, further education, managing a family and home or a job. Do we have sufficient work-life balance in what we do? The answer probably lies in how content we feel, whether we feel stressed or pressurised and if we feel we have time for the things in life which we find to be important. Check out whether you have enough time away from work and the dreaded emails or calls, especially late at night.

We need to keep learning and developing to maintain wellbeing or we start to get stagnant or left behind. What can we do to continually learn something about our world, our work lives or how to develop as a person? This might include developing better people skills, understanding how to be more empathic or simply learning more about how we are, who we are and why we behave the way we do.

How do we cope with problems or issues? Do we have a strategy for managing life issues or do we simply deal with things as they crop up? Would it help us to plan how to respond to adversity in advance? We're not always going to be able to anticipate problems, so a degree of flexibility will always be required.

Our own personal wellness toolkit needs to be individualised with the ingredients that reflect the recipe of our life; our circumstances, the variables which impact our life and world, our family and work situation, our interests and the different demands and pressures on us. It'll also need adapting regularly in order to respond to changes and the consequences of the many things in life out of our control.

Top Tips

Connection
Find time to be with others and socialise. This might include family and friends, as well as those with whom we share interests, sports, hobbies and activities

Relaxation
What chills you out? For some it's a bath, others it's music or hobbies. Or is it going for a walk, reading a book, computer games, watching TV,

cooking, shopping, gardening and so on. Anything which allows your mind to unwind and relax. Don't forget spiritual activities here which can help us get beyond our own immediate problems and give a different perspective to meaning and purpose.

Activation

You don't need to exercise just because it's important to stay fit and healthy. Exercise allows you to work out your anger, frustrations or angst, or to set yourself targets, gain a sense of achievement or to clear your head. It's a mind and body experience.

Journal

Try writing a summary of your day or the thoughts which punctuate it. Aim to find three positive things which have happened, or achievements reached in the day, however small. At the end of the week, you'll have 21. A journal can help you reflect on things as well as transfer thoughts from mind to paper, which, in itself, can help you let go of preoccupying thoughts.

Outdoors

Getting outside allows you to breath fresh air, feel the wind on your face, hear noise and sounds and essentially connect with all your senses. Look up at the things you normally might miss. Stay and be mindful.

Music maestro

Music has a huge impact on mood. As well as triggering memories of sadness, it can elevate and lighten mood too. What are the pieces of music which inspire, motive and nourish you, as well as contributing to making you feel good?

Ask for help

We can't solve and resolve everything on our own. Who can you select as part of your Dream Team for support; those you can call upon to buck you up, help you reconnect, or offer you a shoulder to cry on. If you don't have anyone specific, there are some excellent free national charity helplines, such as the Samaritans in the UK or you may have access to a coach or therapist.

Fun

Life can be very serious. List the activities which you consider to be fun; the things which make you laugh and make you feel good—a comedian you can watch online, an amusing book you can read, people you can laugh with, a TV programme and so on? Smile like you mean to go on.

Ditch the dirt

Negativity can pull us down. How can you rid yourself of the stuff which hangs over you, which distracts and preoccupies you? Take control of any negativity over you or change how you feel, think or respond to it. Avoid negative people or those who drain positivity from you.

Enhance the positive

We all have tasks and activities which make us feel good. Do more of it and find more of it.

Action Plan 38: Your Personal Wellness COMRADE

We all need a comrade, or friend, to help us.

Use the following COMRADE acronym to plot out the Wellness Toolkit which works for you.

Reflect on each letter.

C Connect with others

WHO _____

O Outdoors to be mindful

WHERE _____

M Music to lighten your mood

WHAT _____

R Relax with the things which chill you out

   WHAT _____

A Ask for Help

   WHO _____

D Ditch negativity

   How _____

E Enhance positivity

   How _____

39

Pain Management

Spotlight

The perception of pain can be influenced by a number of factors—past experiences of pain, culture and beliefs, stoicism, anxiety and depression. But to manage pain, we need to understand what it is.

In acute pain, an injury sends a pain message to the brain that something is wrong. This may relate to broken bones, sprains, childbirth, labour, toothache and severe bruising. Acute pain encourages us to immobilise the affected area to aid recovery and rehabilitation.

When it happens, we often experience acute pain as severe but this can reduce in intensity relatively promptly. This is facilitated by becoming aware of progress, improvement and recovery, all of which can help to reduce the effects of pain symptoms.

If acute pain is not sufficiently managed, it can lead to chronic pain. Although chronic pain can sometimes have no clear reason, it does not mean it is 'all in our head'. Ways to manage acute pain, such as with an injury are quite different to managing chronic pain. These injuries are usually best addressed at the Hospital Emergency Department or via the doctor.

Chronic pain lasts for longer than three months and is associated with a repetitive, ongoing or long-term pain issue, such as back pain, regular migraines and severe headaches, cancer, arthritis and nerve-related damage. The enduring nature of chronic pain can make the experience of pain much worse especially if there is no respite in sight or there is no explanation for why the pain is there.

Some people just learn to accept chronic pain, aware that nothing can be done. But others end up on the slippery slope of prescribed medication which is not always helpful as these can have side effects which interfere with and suppress the body's normal functions. They can certainly help but taken excessively or in an uncontrolled way, they can become addictive.

Whilst we talk about acute and chronic pain as a physical manifestation, we need to recognise the crucial impact on mental health and how pain affects us emotionally and psychologically. Physical pain can be triggered by psychological pain. Traumas from the past and present can act as a message conduit for pain. There's frequently a two-way inter-relationship between physical and psychological pain, one impacts the other.

Trying to determine the source of pain can be difficult as the brain can receive conflicting messages. For instance, a pain in our left foot might actually be due to referred pain from a hip problem. Migraines might emerge because of unresolved stress or referred pain from a neck strain. Back pain might be triggered by poor posture, shoes, stress, disrupted sleep, poor diet, excessive alcohol consumption, smoking, inappropriate or a lack of exercise, or even that pain in the left foot.

When we are in pain, we often want acknowledgement, empathy and understanding. We want to be looked after, to be cared for, to be appreciated, heard and listened to. Sure, if we have a leg in plaster and stagger round in crutches, we clearly have some leg issue going on. However, much pain is often invisible to others.

Top Tips

Medical support

Management of acute pain, for example ankle sprain, is different from chronic pain. If you sustain an injury or have pain for no apparent reason, consult with a doctor or visit your local Emergency Department.

Non-prescription medication

There's a reason why medications such as Paracetamol, Aspirin and Ibuprofen are regarded as 'wonder drugs'. They can be very effective as pain relief (under the correct direction) and just because they are available without prescription doesn't mean they are no good.

Accept pain

Once you accept you will have good days and bad days, and ups and downs, you can start to acclimatise and adjust to the changes which occur. Accept your pain and you won't be fighting against it all the time. An acceptance strategy is used in many chronic pain-management clinics as a way to take the pressure off trying to find the solution all the time, when the answer is managing the impact, rather than trying to manage the pain itself.

Pain cycle

The pain cycle starts with the initial pain, then triggers anxiety, which disrupts sleep, leading to increased catastophising, which enhances pain and sets the cycle back in motion again.

Medical resolution

When we visit a doctor or hospital, we tend to assume they will cure us of our ailment. They'll do their best, but there's never any guarantee. Surgery is not always the best option and can make matters worse and pain more chronic. Always seek professional medical advice and second opinions.

Boundaries and limitations

Understand what your limits are. How far can you go before you more hit your pain threshold? Also, with the aid of medical advice, understand what an acceptable or manageable pain is and what is not. You need to find your pain baseline.

Relaxation and exercise

With medical support, advice and supervision, where appropriate, find out what rest you need and also how exercise might actually reduce your pain. In some cases, you need to build up muscle regions to take pressure off joints and bones such as with the aid of physiotherapy or pilates, but as every situation is different, do seek advice. Learning to relax in the right way is important too, for instance swimming might be better than sitting on a sofa with your feet up watching TV.

Getting older

We all age, so do our bodies. We can't necessarily do, or get away with doing, what we did when we were much younger. Accept your limitations and look after your body, rather than abusing it. As you get older, you'll appreciate even more what you have invested into looking after your body.

Pain-management programmes

For more chronic pain issues, there may be pain-management clinics offering pain-management programmes in your locality. Check with your doctor or healthcare professional.

Individual Pain Management

Most pain-management clinicians advocate and recommend that the solution is about how you manage your pain. Get to know it; causes, consequences and cures. What helps, what hinders? It's your body. Medication may help, but it might not cure and beware of the long-term effects of medication such as opioid pain killers which can be highly addictive. Assess what's physical and what might be psychological. Change how you perceive or think about your pain. Can you change your attitude towards pain? Would changing attitudes of others impact how you experience pain, that is do you need your pain to be recognised differently?

Action Plan 39: Personal Pain Profile

To build up your Personal Pain Profile (PPP), you need to define and differentiate what pain means to you. You can then track your scores to understand the variables that impact improving or worsening pain. With this intelligence, you can make changes to your lifestyle and ultimately learn to better manage your own pain. This refers more to chronic, longer-term pain.

Pain Management

1) Identify and adapt how you experience pain, using a 1–10 scale (use your words)
   1. No Pain.
   2. Pain is around but negligible.
   3. Pain is evident if I think about it.
   4. Pain is irritating or bothersome, but I can pretty much ignore it.
   5. Pain is annoying, but I can function OK.
   6. Pain is annoying and is distracting me and affecting concentration.
   7. Pain is really annoying and consumes by thinking but I can still function.
   8. Pain is now severe, impacting my functioning and preoccupying my thinking and sleep.
   9. Pain is making me delirious, distracted, in a right state, out of control.
   10. Pain is excruciating and the worse it can be, I can't function or move.

2) Keep a pain diary, hourly or daily, and describe what you are doing or how you are feeling. At the same time ascribe a pain score from your personalised pain scale—see example.

Example:

Monday	Tuesday	Wednesday	Thursday	Friday	Saturday	Sunday
Walk	Cleaning	Rest	Gardening	Ironing	Walk	Rest
4	6	2	7	5	4	2

Monday	Tuesday	Wednesday	Thursday	Friday	Saturday	Sunday

3) Monitor, assess and review (with medical support, as helps) the times your pain scale fluctuates and how you can adapt your lifestyle to reduce your pain. Notice that your pain scale does change depending on your mood or what you are doing. For instance, you might be less aware of your pain when you are engrossed in an enthralling TV drama!

40

Coping with Illness

Spotlight

We all get coughs and colds now and again. If we're really unlucky, we may experience an illness or injury which incapacitates us for a short period of time. And if we're incredibly unlucky, we'll suffer a more chronic, catastrophic or terminal illness.

Taking the regular colds and flu first, we need to rest and let it work through our bodies. There is little truth to the claim that you 'feed a cold and starve a fever', meaning when you still need to hydrate yourself with plenty of fluids, eat a sensible, balanced nutritious diet and get enough rest.

We can't advise you on the most appropriate medical advice to take for the widespread illnesses we get. When it comes to your physical or mental health, your doctor should be your first point of contact for guidance and advice.

There may be some psychosomatic aspect to our illness, meaning that a physical illness can be exacerbated, triggered, caused or influenced by psychological factors, such as stress and anxiety. How we think can impact how we physically feel. If we are in a depressed state, or feel down, lethargic and lacking of energy, it's likely we may stoop, crouch and drag ourselves. If we feel stressed and uptight, we could have physical tensions in our back, neck and shoulders. How we approach and deal with illnesses psychologically can have a noticeable impact on recovery and rehabilitation.

It's one thing to personally manage our own afflictions and illnesses, but it's quite different if we are supporting a loved one or family member through their illness. We have to contend with their unique perspective and the pain and frustration they may be feeling. It's impossible to fully grasp the impact on others. We can only do what we can to support, sympathise and empathise with their plight and experience of their condition.

What's common for all, is the sense that we are confronted with new limitations to what we used to do before and it's this change which can be tough to manage. When you're not feeling in good form, it can be difficult to summon up a positive and creative perspective on managing limitations.

There might also be feelings of loss…, loss of the healthy and able self. You may also feel anger, frustration, disbelief, depression and low-mood, apathy and loss of motivation and moving towards a clarification, acceptance and recovery. We're left with loads of questions;

'Why me?', 'Why did I have that accident', 'Why was I in the wrong place at the wrong time?', 'Why did I get that cancer diagnosis',' I don't deserve this', 'It's so unfair', 'I just can't believe this is happening to me'.

We hear of things happening to other people but not us. And then it does.

Top Tips

Information, information, Information

You need to know what's going on. What is the diagnosis and what does it mean for you, your partner, family, work and so on? What is the prognosis and what are the implications to you and those around you? Once you have information, you can start to process it and consider the impacts. Get accurate information from your doctor, medical advisor or consultant, with a second opinion, if appropriate.

Understanding, understanding, understanding

It's one thing to work towards knowing what your condition is but learning more about it can give you some context and meaning. It is part of you and you are part of it. Understanding and learning more can help shift some of the sense of it controlling you, to you taking some control back.

Medical Dream Team

Built a network of 'experts' into your care team. You might have several people who are part of your rehabilitation—consultant, doctor, physiotherapist, psychotherapist, psychologist, pain nurse, practice nurse, therapist, coach and so on. Don't assume that the most senior person knows everything. An experienced nurse may have greater knowledge and intuition than a consultant. Trust needs to be earned on behalf of you.

Self-concept changes

You might find that your sense of self or who are you may change. The condition may require you to make adaptations to what had previously been your regular way of living. You may look, feel, behave or think differently. You're adapting to a different way of living. Adaptation becomes the new normal.

Guilt and blame

There can be strong feelings of guilt and blame; maybe you're to blame (or at least that's the way you point your finger), or healthcare professionals who didn't spot the signs, or someone else. There could also be feelings of shame and embarrassment as you adjust to how others see you or regard you, especially if they see you as defined by the illness.

Avoid the Internet

Whilst there are some excellent online resources, it's easy to self-diagnose in error, to become highly anxious as we read about the worst case scenarios or to assume we are afflicted by a condition which does not reflect our situation. Resist internetting and only use websites which are established and trusted. If in doubt check with your doctor.

Take control

The medical profession cannot always cure, treat or resolve everything, and yet we have this blind faith that they have all the answers. Sometimes, your own self-care and self-managing will enable you to take more control and responsibility. This is not to say that you shouldn't listen to the professionals, rather don't assume there's a medical solution to every illness or that they will know everything.

Friends and family

Build a network round you of as many people who can support you. It's unlikely you will get one person looking after you 24/7, so pool that social reservoir of people who can chip in and make a difference. It'll also give you variety having more people to connect with.

Depression and anxiety

If your condition requires Herculean efforts to maintain a normal level of functioning, little things can now seem major. Look out for signs of depression creeping in or for an increasingly frequency level of anxiety and panic. You need to re-calibrate your emotional thermometer and learn to manage the emotions you may experience which you didn't before.

Help

Reach out to others and ask for help. Most people like to be asked for help as it makes them feel good. And so by asking, it might make you feel good too. Win-win. However, be careful that you don't adopt a 'sick role' where you are over-reliant on others. Maintain what you can do by yourself.

Acceptance

You do need to accept how things are for you. This takes the pressure off needing to resolve everything when it just might not be possible. There's no point trying to drive a car at 100 miles per hour if it can only go 70. Accept that the car goes up to 70 miles per hour and you'll have a different, more positive and real relationship with it.

Action Plan 40: Rehabilitation and Recovery Rescue

Having others around you will make you feel more positive about your recovery. Plot all the people, with their email and phone contacts, who can help influence your rehabilitation and/or recovery.

Doctor

Email address: _____

Phone number: _____

Nurse

Email address: _____

Phone number: _____

Best friend

Email address: _____

Phone number: _____

Best family member

Email address: _____

Phone number: _____

Consultant

Email address: _____

Phone number: _____

Physiotherapist

Email address: _____

Phone number: _____

Coach, counsellor or therapist

Email address: _____

Phone number: _____

Add yours _____

Email address: _____

Phone number: _____

Add yours _____

Email address: _____

Phone number: _____

Add yours _____

Email address: _____

Phone number: _____

Add yours _____

Email address: _____

Phone number: _____

Add yours _____

Email address: _____

Phone number: _____

Plot out your weekly appointments, medications needed and positive activities to keep you healthy.

Section III

Personal Resilience

41

Personal Fulfilment, Satisfaction and Purpose

Spotlight

Society has a preoccupation with the need 'to be happy' and yet this is a somewhat abstract and simplistic concept. Happiness is arbitrary and potentially superficial. What defines and triggers happiness can change from day to day, person to person and context to context.

But a deeper and often more longer-lasting construct of happiness is found in fulfilment and purpose. These are more powerful drivers which fuel ambition, determination and focus. A motor vehicle might have a nice shiny exterior, but ultimately what's inside and under the bonnet is where it all happens.

What is the engine that drives us? We'll each have a different engine. We'll be influenced by our background, family, education, affluence, location, spiritual perspective and work. And yet despite a complex matrix of variables there are some commonalities.

Abraham Maslow (1943, 1954) constructed a hierarchy of needs to explain a theory of human motivation. Often demonstrated in a pyramid diagram, Maslow hypothesised a sequential order for meeting human needs, though they don't have to be completed to move to the next level;

Biological and physiological needs—shelter, water, food, clothing. Safety and resourcing needs—personal safety and security, employment, accommodation. Love and belonging—intimacy, partnerships, friendships, belonging, social connection. Esteem and self-worth—respect, trust, honest, self-esteem, dignity, reputation. Self-actualising—realising personal potential and the best we can be

William Glasser (2001) evolved his 'Choice Theory' to suggest that psychological turmoil exists when one need or choice conflicts with another and that resolution is achieved by making more informed need-satisfying choices.

This leaves us to consider that what fulfils us is both a mitigation of potential conflict and the pursuit of a place of positive nourishment. Ultimately, we need to find our own definition of fulfilment, satisfaction and purpose. They're personal projections, ambitions and objectives. They're constructs we strive to achieve and absorb into our way of being. But there's usually a trade-off along the way as we negotiate the relationship between each. Meaning and purpose are moral drivers which form the bedrock of our personality and we build fulfilment and satisfaction from this foundation.

Society and laws may impose a moral compass on us, but ultimately we have to appreciate, agree with and understand the substance to this. This creates a cultural norm which guides expectations of behaviour, and yet even with this, we have our own personal definition of what motivates and inspires us. Once we start to gain spiritual, physical and psychological nourishment, the cycle starts to repeat itself, so we start to crave more spiritual, physical and psychological 'food'.

Top Tips

Daily purpose

Why do you get up in the morning? What stops you staying in bed all day? It might be your need to get to work so you can earn a living, but there will be an underlying purpose behind this. Why are you working? Is it to provide for your family, to save up for a deposit on a house, to get money to travel or for your pension?

Job and work
Why do you do what you do? What choices helped inform and direct you into this role? Where could you go with this, including different angles or perspectives?

Wants and needs
Differentiate between how you define a 'want' and a 'need'. Your needs will often define values and purpose whereas your wants may be more superfluous and negotiable.

Choice and control
You have responsibility for no one except yourself. You have ultimate control over what you say, think, believe and feel. Make your choices with respect for yourself and others.

Transparency
Your openness to the world around you will amplify your purpose and meaning. How do you 'live' what you believe or are you all talk and no action? Be true and congruent to yourself and others around you and you're more likely to find this replicated back to you.

What matters?
When something conflicts with something which is important to us we can feel stressed, anxious or depressed. But these are also powerful signs of exactly what is important to us. If it doesn't bother us much, they're not that important.

Delay gratification
It can be tempting to fall victim to short-termism and want a quick-fix or seek more instant gratification. But learning to delay gratification increases the value, reward and achievement.

Spirituality
Whether you call this a religion, philosophy or spirituality, what drives you to a higher moral purpose? What defines your construct of spirituality? If you don't have one, why not explore this?

Fate

Do you believe everything is predefined and determined for you or do you feel you need to shape the future? Whatever you believe, you may be missing out on the opportunities which you can create or if it is predetermined, making the most of every opportunity.

Action Plan 41: 'What Is Important to Me' Template

Understanding why things are important to us helps shape and determine what fulfils, nourishes and satisfied us. It also enables us to appreciate our repertoire of needs and wants.

Write down WHY each one of the following prompts is important to you.

If you struggle to define a clear reason for a particular prompt, this might suggest a deficiency which needs attention. But it might also illustrate you simply assign limited importance to that prompt. There's no right or wrong answer—we offer this template to give you food for thought.

- Partner _____
- Social relationships _____
- Friends _____
- Family _____
- Current job _____
- Work colleagues _____
- Career/work _____
- Affluence _____
- Pesonal safety _____
- Personal development _____
- Spiritual enlightenment _____
- Belonging _____
- Personal identity _____

Personal Fulfilment, Satisfaction and Purpose

- Reputation _____
- Fashion _____
- Entertainment _____
- Creativity _____
- Music _____
- Art _____
- Likeability _____
- Companionship _____
- Trust _____
- Respect _____
- Loyalty _____
- Love _____
- Learning _____
- Dignity _____
- Privacy _____
- Humour _____
- Fun _____
- Excitement _____
- Experiences _____

42

Work-Life Balance

Spotlight

'Work', in this context, refers to a range of activities including employment, looking for work, academic studies, caring for dependants and running a home. This is different to the 'Life' bit, which relates to the fun stuff we do, or the hobbies and interests we pursue, or the activities which connect with our value or belief system which inspires, motivates, enthuses and nourishes us.

But what is the right balance? There's no right or wrong here, simply what works for us and our situation. What one person considers as an appropriate balance might be a nightmare scenario for someone else. We choose what's important to our life and why.

Work does vacuum up a huge amount of our waking hours. Approximately we sleep for 8 hours, work for 8 hours and use the remaining 8 hours to commute and do all the other bits and pieces in between. The reality, however, is that work and our commute can take up 10–12+ hours, we sleep less than we need and the balance is spent recalibrating our headspace. This means that some of the important aspects of our lives are depleted, under-nourished or ignored.

Sure, work gives us a reason to get up in the morning, it gives us purpose, meaning, focus, a work persona, an income, a sense of community and connection, a passion and drive, motivation and inspiration and captivation. But it can also sap all our efforts and energy so that we lose sight of some of the crucial aspects that make us whole.

It's not all about work. But it is all about us and knowing how to get a balance. Certainly all play and no work can get boring or aimless. Our reality is more often than not, all work and no play.

Top Tips

Work assessment

What do you enjoy about or get from your work? Is it just the wage packet at the end of the month? What about the actual work you do, your work colleagues, the learning and development you gain, or the new work skills you practice, acquire and use, the prospects of career promotion or enhancement, developing a longer career plan? What about voluntary work? What would that mean or give to you?

Ambition

What is your ambition and what does it mean to you and why does it matter? Is it to reach a certain level of job or pay? Is it about a stepping stone to a new career path? Are you happy where you are and content to stay put? Do you need more responsibility, excitement, challenge, inspiration or reward?

Quality not quantity

We all waste a lot of time at work with pointless meetings, idle conversations, online distractions including social media, repetitions and duplications of effort and discussions that take far longer than need be. Can you work smarter? Having said this, there may be some important social interaction which occurs during these more superfluous communications. It's also about building relationships, developing trust and respect, seeking our assurances and allegiances.

Multi-task or focus

Do you need to multi-task to keep you stimulated or can you only focus on one thing at a time? We all have a bit of one or the other in us but this means that we may face challenges if and when this style changes. Establish whether you like to juggle or whether this dilutes your focus.

Boundary work and home

Most of us have a separated work and home life. But for many, particularly those self-employed or working from home, this can blur. Keeping a tight boundary between work and home helps us to achieve more of a balance. We might be tempted to talk about work at home or our home-lives at work but what benefit does this serve? Does our partner really want to hear about our colleague's faltering work presentation and does our work colleague really need to know every high and low of our seven-year-old son?

Health and fitness

The world has an obesity problem. And it's getting bigger. Much of this is associated with an increased sedentary lifestyle and lack of exercise. We know that exercise helps to release the body's natural feel-good hormones as well as increasing our sense of wellbeing. Fitness can be a personal quest or something which provides a social connection through team sports. Small steps can make a difference including using the stairs rather than an elevator, or having a daily walk. Even when we know we should keep more active and fitter, often the excuse is that we don't have time.

Creativity bounds

We all have some creativity within us, whether it's related to sports, activities, music, arts, dance, drawing and so on, but we often don't regard these as creative. It's about connecting with our imagination and how we use a creative expression to make a different sense of the world around us.

Social life

As social creatures, humans need interactions with others, whether they're work colleagues, friends or family. It doesn't have to involve hours of conversation, it can just be about being connected with others, such as going to a sporting event or music gig, taking a walk, shopping together, going to the pub or a café, sharing exercise or dog walking, groups, society and clubs and so on.

Money management

Do you know how much money you have in your bank account at this precise moment? Do you know your monthly outgoings against your income? Are you earning enough to meet your financial commitments? If you are, then great. If not, do you prioritise the right options to change your financial status?

Relationships

How much value do you attribute to your close relationships—partners, family, parents and significant others? And how much time do you invest in these relationships? Most people say 'not enough'?

Gimme Love

How much love do you get? How much love do you give? Do you need love? Most people say 'not enough'!

Spiritual sustenance

About two-thirds of the world's population have a religious faith, with some societies much more so than others. Spirituality may cover faith and religion but it can also include a belief or value system which is neither religious nor faith-based. Whether you describe yourself as spiritual or religious, what time do you give to the beliefs or values you hold?

Havin' Fun

What is fun? Having a laugh, sharing happy experiences, feeling content? It probably doesn't really matter how we define it, as long as we get enough of it. Often we max out on work or expectations or family commitments and miss or lose out on the fun parts of life. We know we're having fun because if feels good.

Action Plan 42: Work-Life Balance Matrix

Please consider each of the eight work-life areas and consider how much satisfaction you currently derive from each. Circle the number score which applies.

Date: _____

How satisfied are you with your work/life- balance?

	Not satisfied							Very satisfied	
Career & Work	1	2	3	4	5	6	7	8	9
Finances & Money	1	2	3	4	5	6	7	8	9
Partner & Romance	1	2	3	4	5	6	7	8	9
Family & Friends	1	2	3	4	5	6	7	8	9
Social Life & People Contact	1	2	3	4	5	6	7	8	9
Health & Fitness	1	2	3	4	5	6	7	8	9
Fun & Recreation	1	2	3	4	5	6	7	8	9
Creativity & Personal Growth	1	2	3	4	5	6	7	8	9

The lower score for each item, the more attention might be required to create a better work-life balance. Each time you complete this Action Plan, monitor and review your scores so you can assess and react to decreases accordingly.

What changes do you need to make to achieve the satisfaction levels which you require?

_____

_____

_____

43

Personal and Professional Development

Spotlight

In resilience terms, personal and professional development is concerned with acquiring skills and competencies to enhance our knowledge and understanding, and in so doing become better adept and resourced to tackle all the tasks, demands, challenges and stresses which life throws at us.

Life is an ongoing journey of learning and each and every experience we encounter feeds into our memory bank of life management. Some of this may be positive, and some of this may be less positive, but it's how we interpret and learn from these experiences which matters.

Professional development is concerned with learning to improve the skills we need to carry out the work we engage with in our profession or chosen field of work. This acquisition of skills may come from learning to do our job better over time or it may be from learning from others, such as a mentor or going on courses and training events. We may wish to improve our capabilities to make our job easier or because we would like to advance our job prospects or career.

Ultimately though, however adept we become at our job, we may need to draw upon our personal development. These relate to how we advance as a person, through relating and social skills, how we get on with others and how we understand more about our self. Often regarded as 'soft skills' or emotional intelligence, these are often tougher to acquire than the 'hard skills' of job-related competencies.

Our professional development will be significantly influenced by the profession we work in, the job we have and our career stage. Budgets and resources will impact too, as will the capacity for us to identify and find the right learning plans and the people who can offer support and influence.

People are crucial to our professional development. We can learn all we need to know to do our job, but without people we may struggle to apply it and advance in our work. We need the collaboration, encouragement and nurturing of others. There's always a turn-over of staff in any organisation as people leave or retire. Opportunities may emerge or we may need to leave to find the opportunities. Finding someone senior to us who is willing and able to mentor us can provide this bridge to advancement.

Mentoring emerges as the subset between professional and personal development as it allows us to learn the key work skills needed for the job, whilst also finding out about the more implicit norms and rules involved in 'getting on' with others and knowing the politics and mechanics of 'how things are done' in an organisation.

Nothing stands still at work or home. Change is all around us. If we do nothing, we stagnate or get left behind. Personal and professional development allows us to acquire the skills to meet these changes and be better equipped to deal with them. At work, it might be adapting to advances in information technology, legislation and processes, and in a non-work environment, it could be learning how to manage our emotions better, or respond to stressful situations, or become better adept at relationship building.

Top Tips

Anticipate change

To keep ahead of the game, you need to know how the game might change. History can influence trends but you need to tolerate the ambiguity of things changing in an unexpected way.

Future responsibilities

What skills will you need for the future, whether this is in your relationships at home or work, as a parent or a manager? You will have some idea how things are going to map out. Prepare for them before you need them.

Keep updated

What do you need to know that you don't know? Is technology creeping in which will change how you work (or engage with your children)? Is legislation going to impact government policy, or changes to your finances or your health?

Engagement

How connected are you to what you do, at home and work? If you're always one step behind, then everything will feel more of an effort than it needs to be. How can you engage more with the work you do and people in your life to get a step ahead?

Motivation

What gets you up in the morning or inspires you to do anything? Identify and nurture this enthusiasm as it's going to tap into your positivity and optimism. With motivation comes inspiration and creativity. Find the kernel of your inner-mojo to identify how you can develop this further.

Build on strengths

You're going to be good at some things and less so at others. Forget the latter and play to your strengths. The more you engage with your strengths, the more you'll tap into the powerhouse that drives and develops you.

Manage weaknesses

Why spend an inordinate amount of time on the things you struggle with? Do you really need to be an expert in everything or can you delegate to someone better skilled than you? Managing a weakness can be more effective than trying to eliminate it altogether. Accept your weaknesses by focusing more on what you are good at.

Develop others

By developing and inspiring others, you'll learn more about yourself and the people skills you'll acquire in the process. Watching someone else blossom will encourage you to do more of the same. Their gain is also your gain.

New skills

Only you can know what skills you need to develop. Is it more work-based or personal? What's going to make more of a positive difference to you in your work or at home? Identify the skills and competencies and acquire them, then bask in the reflective knowledge that has been instrumental to your advancement.

Action Plan 43: Personal and Professional Development Roadmap

The following acts as a process flow for any personal or professional development quest:

1. Assess your current capabilities and skills set (work or non-work)

   _____

2. Identify your development needs

   _____

3. Clarify your development needs and expectations

   _____

4. Identify the tasks or skills required to meet your development needs

   _____

5. Carry out your development tasks

   _____

6. Reflect over how you have met your development tasks which have led to outcomes

   _____

7. Consider how these outcomes apply to your work or home life

   _____

8. Review the outcome and whether this is sufficient

   _____

9. Identify and assess any further needs

   _____

10. Begin the process again

    _____

44

Acceptance Strategies

Spotlight

The Serenity Creed or prayer, first scripted by American theologian Reinhold Niebuhr (1892–1971), proposes *'Grant me the courage to change the things I can, the serenity to accept the things I cannot change, and the wisdom to know the difference'*.

We fight against things which we cannot change, in the hope that we can. It is this un-changeable quest which is what causes us the tension, heartache and angst. We seem determined to battle against the odds, challenge science and the laws of probability in the belief that we will win. We are not superhuman, we are simply human.

The Serenity Creed also reflects the courage sometimes required to instigate change and, crucially, the wisdom, insight or understanding to know what we can change and what we cannot. It seems simple, in theory. But in practice we often lose this perspective.

Acceptance and Commitment Therapy emerged (Hayes et al. 1999) as a means by which we can learn acceptance to respond positively to a whole host of issues, including for trauma support and chronic pain management. Fighting or opposing something you cannot change causes unmanageable pain and suffering. By accepting a situation and avoiding resistance, you can start to embrace the choices which emerge from this. You focus your energies to choose to work around your problem or issue rather than against it. Then you act on it. Accept, Choose, Take Action (ACT).

Imagine you get a parking ticket because you stayed longer than your ticket permitted. You are outraged, indignant and horrified. 'How dare they', 'I was only 5 minutes late', 'they MUST cancel the fine, it is totally unfair'. But, you WERE late. You exceeded your time allowance.

You might feel angry and upset (probably more about yourself than anything else), but facts are facts. You can fight them, challenge them or try to change them but consider the stress you will go through with letters, emails, phone calls and so on. Or you can accept it, choose to put it down to bad luck and take action by paying the fine and getting on with your life. Although this is only a simple example, what would you do in this situation and think of the choices you have?

Things which we ruminate over at night and prevent us getting a good sleep often stem from things we are trying to resolve or change but can't. What if we could put all those thoughts into an imaginary little box, lock it up, put it into a filing cabinet down the corridor and leave it there. Then, focus on getting to sleep. For instance, imagine you're worrying about paying for your credit card bill which has just come through. It's totally normal to be concerned about something like that, because it matters and may have consequences. But worrying about it at night won't resolve it or make it go away.

What about accepting you have the bill and that there's nothing (in bed) you can do about it. Write this problem down on a piece of paper, so you shift it from thoughts to paper. Choose to think of something else to aid sleep and commit to giving sufficient time and energy to resolving the problem when you have the time and energy to do so. There's a time and place for everything.

Accept, Choose, Take Action.

Top Tips

Reflection

Consider an issue which has stressed you recently and assess how you could have adopted an acceptance strategy to the situation to mitigate the stress for you.

Future positive

Anticipate something which might happen in the future which could benefit from an acceptance perspective. Work out and through how you will be ready to adopt this strategy in good time.

Rubber inflatable dingy

Imagine you're in a rubber inflatable dingy charging down a dangerously fast-flowing river. You could possibly try and grab branches over the water's edge, but risk capsizing or falling over-board. What if you go with the flow until the water calms?

Change what you can

Acceptance is not about doing nothing. It is part of the active process of deciding what to accept and what to change. Acceptance doesn't prioritise change. Where and when you can, take responsibility, act and change.

Not acceptable

Embracing an 'acceptance strategy' doesn't mean you need to accept what might be unacceptable behaviour or attitudes. What is unacceptable in your place of work, at home, with friends, in relationships and so on remains unacceptable, such as sexual harassment.

Avoid avoidance

The act of avoiding a particular issue, problem or experience because you fear the consequences or outcome doesn't necessarily reduce the threat or subsequent anguish. You may still need to face up or confront difficult situations. Your acceptance strategy may require you to take action.

Count the benefits

Accepting something rather than spending time fighting the impossible will mean you have spare time to dedicate to something more positive or fulfilling. Make a note of this 'new' time and reflect on the time-accrued value in adopting this acceptance strategy.

Connect values

Establishing your value or belief system will help you recognise what gives you meaning and purpose, which in turn will enable you to identify what is important, and significantly, what is not.

Letting go

Once you have decided to stop fighting an issue, let it go, seek closure, mark the turning, embrace the change and move on.

Stay with meaningful

Dispense with the trivial, simplistic and meaningless issues which clutter your mind and focus attention on what is really important to you and the people around you.

Drop the principle

How many times do you hold onto a problem or issue because you are totally determined to resolve it 'out of principle'? Is this really in your best interest to do this and why? What good will this serve, except to reinforce a steely determination and potential stubbornness?

Action Plan 44: Acceptance Plan

Use the Acceptance Plan to chart the various personal issues which you feel you are fighting against or which are causing you stress or distress.

Acceptance Strategies

Issue/Problem	What can you change?	What can you accept?	What choices emerge from acceptance?	What actions do you need to take help accept the situation?

45

Emotional Intelligence

Spotlight

Over 20 years ago, Daniel Goleman championed 'Emotional Intelligence' and claimed it mattered more than cognitive intelligence or IQ. Whilst our education systems have focused on the pursuit of learning and the acquisition of knowledge, our schools, colleges and universities tend not to prize or target the attribution of emotional and people skills.

Emotional intelligence is essentially about being intelligent about our emotions. We all have a repertoire of emotions we express and vent, maybe not always in the right way or at the right time, but it doesn't stop us venting. Being more emotionally intelligent is about being clearer about what we express, why and when. It doesn't block spontaneity or transparency, rather it's about understanding that how we express our emotion affects others as well as ourselves.

There's usually a human component associated with emotional expression, as we're communicating important information to others. It might be that someone else is a cause of our emotional response or we may have a need to express a specific emotional message to another. Perhaps our emotion is signalling that we require a comparable response or reaction from others, such as seeking reassurance, or clarification, or love and affection, or praise and adulation, or an apology and so on.

We're not taught how to get on with people, yet throughout our lives we're thrown into a boiling cauldron of personalities and meant to find our way and define our own identity in the process. Most of the stresses we experience at home or at work involve relationships, yet again, we're not taught how to be in relationship with others.

Building effective relationships is a journey of life-long learning, and one that ebbs and flows depending on the groups we pass through, the bonds we make and the chords we cut. Life can be about building together new friends, contacts and acquaintances as much as ditching the ones who are not good for us and generate tension and conflict in our worlds. But, at home and work, we might not have the luxury of being able to 'release' contact with people so we have to find a way to get on and build meaningful, positive and functional relationships.

Having an intelligence with our emotions involves understanding how we generate, react to and express our emotions. Where do they come from and why do they surge through us? What message are they trying to tell us? Are they appropriate for the level of intensity expressed? Or are we hiding from our emotions and deluding ourselves behind a façade of masks and barriers? Why do some people seem to let rip with an emotional outburst at the slightest provocation and yet others struggle to find any depth of emotional capacity? And it can change from cultures to societies.

We need to understand how we tick, in order to understand others. Empathy is a major construct of emotional intelligence; 'walking in the shoes of others', understanding their situation and experience from their perspective, not ours. By accurately understanding others, we can learn more about reason and context; why someone is saying what they do or feeling what they emote.

To have no emotional expression, communication and dialogue renders us robots. Emotions are fundamental to being human and how we successfully connect and engage with our world (or not).

Top Tips

Emotional awareness

Take an average working week and monitor and track your moods and emotions over this period. Pay attention to the highs and lows, when you're stressed or relaxed. Include what's happening before and after each emotion point, in order to understand what you're reacting to, when and how.

Emotions management/regulation

As you track your emotional awareness, monitor the appropriateness of each emotional response. Is it accurate and in proportion? How do you define this? You can create more or less impact by varying the tempo of your emotional reaction. Some people want to be less 'emotional' or find ways to express emotions more. Which one are you and why?

Emotional consequences

You may have a right or a need to jump up and down in anger, but what are the consequences for you doing so in the short-term situation and on the relationships involved?

Knowing me, knowing you

How does understanding yourself help you to understand what's going on for others? Can you reflect on situations which other people are going through or struggling with and where you can identify with a similar experience? How did you respond and how are they reacting?

Empathic awareness

Suspend judgement and your own 'stuff' and walk in the experience of others. What are they thinking, feeling or doing and why are they choosing these options over alternatives?

Active listening

Listen behind the words and look out for non-verbal cues such as body language and the things that communicate a lot but which are not conveyed in words. Listen intently, reflecting your understanding and communicating what you have heard. We don't like it when we feel we haven't been heard. We usually repeat ourselves until we have the confirmation.

Dangers with parallel talking

Someone says 'I'm frustrated', you respond with 'I was frustrated yesterday'. You have not only failed to acknowledge the person, but you have seized the conversation and taken it over. Parallel-talking is two different conversations going on at once and rarely works.

Relationship management

Relationships are not just two-way interactions, but the relationship takes on an entity in its own right, so it's actually a three-way concept. However, you can only take 50% credit, blame and responsibility for an effective relationship.

Motivation

What inspires you to do anything? How do you motivate yourself, keep optimistic and stay positive? Identify what's intrinsic motivation (what drives you from within) and what's extrinsic (e.g. salary or feeling that you 'should' do something as it is expected). Intrinsic motivations are usually more powerful.

Self-responsibility

You, and only you, are responsible for how you express yourself and communicate with others. This takes self-control, self-awareness and self-management. It's not to stop a freedom of spontaneity but to check that you have taken notice of accountability.

Action Plan 45: Self-awareness Audit

Reflect back to a recent experience when you became aware of your emotional response:

(a) Define and deconstruct the emotional response, for example frustration, with anger and annoyance.

(b) What happened in the lead up to, or in the moment of, your emotional response?

_____

(c) What three alternative emotional responses could you have chosen?

1. _____
2. _____
3. _____

(d) Why did you express what you did and why not choose the alternatives?

_____

(e) What can you learn to do differently next time?

_____

(f) Reflect how you have expanded your knowledge and understanding of your personal emotional repertoire.

_____

46

Assertiveness

Spotlight

Assertiveness is the skill, art or ability to assert oneself. That's the simple definition, but the execution or delivery of this can be much more complex. We will all have been influenced by the assertiveness skills (or lack) of our parents, significant others, friends and teachers when we were growing up and we will have been tainted by difficulties they might have had in relation to assertiveness.

There's often a confusion about assertiveness and a host of influencing emotions or behaviours, such as how we express anger, or attitudes to aggression or fear of conflict or simply being unclear how to deal with 'strong' messages from other people. If we're not very assertive, then being on the receiving end of an assertiveness person may be misinterpreted as aggressive or arrogance.

It also links with our self-worth and self-confidence. If we feel strong about ourselves and the value we place on our rights to communicate and assert ourselves, we may be OK, but if we feel we are timid, shy or have low self-worth, we may give up self-control and empower others at our expense.

Many of us have distinct memories of people in authority, such as a parent or teacher, who intimidated or scared us with their assertive style, which we have since interpreted as threatening behaviour. And with any sense of threat, we can naturally retreat. We might then fall into a behaviour pattern of being fearful of authority, of being judged or of being criticised.

We might also feel guilty about asserting ourselves, finding it difficult to say 'No'. The guilt often comes from an ill-conceived impression that saying 'No' will make the other person judge us unfairly, consider us to be weak or not like us. This need to be liked or appear strong can make us over-compensate; trying to please the other person to our detriment. But we're important in all this too.

Sometimes we may feel that being assertive is selfish or somehow self-centred. We are putting our own needs before the needs of others. But what's wrong with that? Are we not better able to help or meet the needs of others when we're in a stronger position of having had our needs met first?

When people speak loudly or hog the conversation, they can come across as oppressive or controlling, but it might also mask other issues they have; their need to be heard, their need to be liked, their need to be in control. Or, in some cases, people who speak loudly do so because they have partial deafness—it's much more common than we appreciate. But the point is, there can be reasons why others behave the way they do, and it's often about them masking their limitations, not an intentional focus on squashing or belittling us.

Being assertiveness is about choice; a choice over how and when to communicate in a way which meets our needs or what's appropriate in a given situation. For instance, it's not always about shouting the loudest. People who speak with a quiet voice, pausing for impact, can often be heard the loudest. We're important. What we have to say or communicate is important too.

Top Tips

Understand your emotions

When you have a sufficient insight and awareness of your emotional repertoire, you will be better able to regulate when and how to engage, allow or ventilate the appropriate emotions. For instance, how do you express sadness or joy or frustration or anger, rather than keeping it 'inside' you and suppressing a normal human emotion?

Belief, purpose and meaning

What is important to you and why? What gives you drive, purpose or meaning? What do you or would you stand up for? What do you have strong opinions about and why?

Tension awareness

Sometimes when we're tense, we can be masking, supressing or depressing something. Use your tension barometer to become alert to your signs of tension, the cause or source and what you need to do, and say, to express yourself appropriately.

Communication steps

What is one thing you can do differently or that you can change, which will improve how you say what you say or to better say when you mean? This might include being open with your emotions, or negative thoughts you have, such as being able to say to someone 'I'm feeling really frustrated', or 'that behaviour annoys me' or 'I can't stop thinking about what X said to me' and so on.

Reality check

If you find you reign in assertiveness because you think doing so will make people not like you, test it. Is that really going to happen? What's the probability someone won't like you if you assert yourself? Pretty low. If, for whatever reason, they end up not liking you, it's very unlikely to be because you asserted yourself. And it might be more about their issues than you.

Anger and aggression

Understand your own attitudes, beliefs and behaviours towards anger and aggression. We're never taught how to express anger, we just learn from others, and not necessarily from the best examples. Is it about unfairness, something unjust, inappropriate? Is it about how someone is made to feel? When is anger appropriate and when not? Is aggression ever positive? When you start to understand your own impulses, you'll be better able to grasp anger in others.

Manage situations

In which situations do you struggle with being assertiveness? Is it with your boss, your partner, your parent and so on? What do you fear here or what's the perceived threat to you? Does this person remind you of someone from the past who has skewed or damaged your ability to assert yourself?

Play to strengths

Most of us are assertive in some situations, perhaps reigning in a disobedient pet or protecting a child from danger. Understand why you are able to be assertive here and why this is OK for you. How can you transfer this personal strength and inner assertiveness to other situations?

Change your beliefs

If you believe it's selfish, rude, arrogant, embarrassing or unnecessary to be assertive, then you're already fighting to justify your right to be assertive. If you believe that at times it is necessary, appropriate and healthy to assert yourself, you will be. What are your belief blocks and what new beliefs about assertiveness do you need to embrace?

Action Plan 46: Take the Assertiveness Challenge

Consider the examples below and try out as many as you feel comfortable attempting.

Monitor when you successfully achieve each example and the positive feelings this creates in you.

Embrace, celebrate and learn from each achievement.

If, however, any of the challenges creates a huge anxiety, stress or panic, take a step back or stop.

It might be helpful to speak to your doctor, coach or therapist to explore why you react in the way you do and what you can do differently.

1. Say NO to someone without apologising.

2. Treat and reward yourself for no specific reason.

3. Tell someone (perhaps, someone you don't know very well) how you are feeling.

4. Express anger when you feel angry.

5. Talk to a shop cashier or teller.

6. Express appreciation and offer thanks for good service.

7. Send food back in a restaurant if you believe it is not cooked the way you want it.

8. Admit when you don't know something.

9. Challenge a person who unfairly criticises you.

10. Ask for constructive criticism and choose what you believe to be helpful and constructive.

11. Admit when you have made a mistake and filter your apology to what is appropriate.

12. Explain to someone an issue which is really important to you.

13. Tell someone they are wrong, when you identify that they are wrong.

14. Criticise someone when you are negatively affected by their behaviour and explain why.

15. Identify when your needs or rights are more important than someone else's.

16. Start a conversation with someone you have not met before.

17. Perform random acts of kindness, for no reason or pay-back.

18. Ask someone for assistance or help without offering to return the favour.

19. Tell someone when they are annoying you and why.

20. Stand up for something you believe in and communicate this to someone.

Add in some additional challenges, so you tailor opportunities to you and your environment.

21. _____

22. _____

23. _____

24. _____

25. _____

Create an assertiveness achievement sheet, folder or book and write about each successful attempt. Reflect back on your achievements regularly so you can reinforce the benefits of your triumphs.

47

Constructive Anger

Spotlight

Constructive anger emphasises that anger, as an emotion, can be good, positive and healthy. It is a primal emotion from early human evolution to help us survive by reacting to danger. Anger is usually a three-stage process; an activating event occurs, our brain seeks to make sense of it or evaluates the threat in order to prepare to react, then we act.

We might also feel anger if we are frustrated, particularly with ourselves, and if we experience an injustice, unfairness, wrongdoing, discrimination, maltreatment or victimisation. It can also be triggered, not just from WHAT someone says to us, such as an insult or undue criticism, but HOW they communicate it. The tone, manner, facial cues and other body language can add significant weight to a verbal message. We can become quite adept at intuitively reading the signs and signals of a message as much as what we hear. And yet we can become attuned to the misreading of such signals too.

The press frequently reports on people in the media limelight who lash out in a fit of anger, either verbally or via threatening social media posts.

We often hear these people are referred for 'anger management' where they learn how to understand anger impulses and the way to channel their emotions in a less destructive manner. In many of these cases, these 'celebrities' are used to having power and control. When they don't get it, their low frustration tolerance kicks in and they kick out.

Just because something doesn't go the way we want it to, doesn't give us the excuse to fire off. This can reflect back to child-like behaviour, unleashing a tantrum to demonstrate frustration or to get something we wanted. If we have very strong core beliefs about what is right and wrong, then we're more likely to experience people or situations which do not conform or subscribe to our belief system; this becomes a threat to our way of being. It's not to take away the right to express anger, but there's a time and a place and this resonates with the value of emotional regulation (being emotionally intelligent enough to know what emotion is appropriate to express at the right time).

Everything seems to be happening faster these days and this feeds our expectation that we want everything now. Media churns out news faster than ever, but can still be eclipsed by social media, where we can now create our own news story before the media has picked up on it. Even supermarkets, including some of the discount retailers, churn us out on a fast-moving conveyor-belt shopping experience. We don't like to wait anymore. Hanging around for public transport or waiting for food in a restaurant can feel like an eternity.

Anger is a tough emotion to appreciate. Not only does it involve understanding our own triggers and pressure points, but it's also about fathoming out the messages and cues from anger directed at us by others. We can easily misinterpret and misunderstand the anger from others, particularly if we have inaccurate or incomplete information. We can be quick to jump to the wrong conclusions. Emails are a classic example, where the brevity and style of communication can often lead to misinterpretation. Lots of people say they don't like confrontation, but it usually translates to not feeling comfortable in potentially volatile situations or not understanding how to manage anger (in us and others).

Top Tips

Anger versus aggression

How can you differentiate between the emotional state of being angry, which is ok, and the behaviour of acting aggressively, which is not ok (unless you are physically defending yourself and have no other options)? Are you trying to prove a point or seek to appear 'strong'? Is this an example of using your 'red mist' to control others?

Acceptance

Accepting that none of us are perfect allows us to appreciate the high standards we expect of ourselves and others might not be reasonable and accurate. What can you accept in others?

Reasoning and facts

Might there be good reasons for inappropriate behaviour? If someone overreacts, what if they've just suffered a bereavement or relationship break-up? If someone speeds past you in a car, might it be a mother fraught to pick up her distressed child? Would that change your response? If you can get a real or better understanding, you'll appreciate the situation differently. Control your angry thoughts until you have all the facts.

Frustration

It's easy to get frustrated. But it's more helpful to tolerate frustration. Possessing a high frustration tolerance will contribute to reduced stress and anger. Next time you feel frustrated, take a few deep breaths and apply some perspective to the situation. But also if you are frustrated, work out why and make a change rather than just sitting on it.

Delay gratification

If you MUST have something now, and don't get it, you will feel disappointment ... and probably frustrated, and consequently angry. But delaying gratification can help to increase appreciation for achievement, success and reward because you've waited for it and have earnt it.

Body check

Feel the effects of your emotional state impacting your body and acknowledge it. Can you feel the difference in bodily reactions when you are feeling angst, or frustrated, or angry or raging? You can modulate your behaviour by checking how your body is responding to difficult situations.

Fight or flight

Anger can be used constructively to deal with an immediate threat by giving us energy and focus. By channelling blood and oxygen to our core organs, we boost our capacity to 'fight or flight', as well as making us temporarily more immune to pain.

Impact of stifling

Bottling up pent-up anger and frustration often means we internalise psychologically, through anxiety and depression, or physically, with high blood pressure, heart problems or digestion problems. If you spot these signs, are you withholding or suppressing your anger?

Exercise

It is difficult to be angry after exercise as the body has discharged the energy which anger often requires to keep it 'hot'. Identify how you can integrate an increased level of activity into your daily routine especially if you lead a sedentary lifestyle.

Stimulants and alcohol

Coffee, tea and tobacco all stimulate the body and mind by acting on neurotransmitters in the brain. These can increase the energy we feel and exacerbate existing feelings of anger. Alcohol is sometimes an elevating stimulant when first consumed although over time, it has a more prominent depressant effect and disturbs the quality of sleep. How do stimulants impact your anger?

Change the situation

Anger can increase when we feel trapped in a situation, perceiving there is no way out. Road rage is a good example; back down and de-escalate the situation. What do you gain or prove by escalating an angry situation? Look for ways to actively remove yourself from a potentially volatile situation, to 'walk away' or take steps to defuse the confrontation.

Breathe out anger

Anger generates arousal feelings where our breathing rate, pulse and heart rate speed up. As feelings of anger emerge, close your eyes or focus your attention on something in the distance and gradually count to ten. 1 – 2 – 3 – 4 notice that your jaw is less tense … 5 – 6 – 7 you become aware of your breathing, try to slow it down… 8 – 9 – 10 you haven't reacted. Now you're calmer, clearer, collected and cooler.

Call in the experts

Breathing management won't solve all anger issues, which could be much more deeper-rooted. Consult with an anger-management specialist, doctor, therapist or coach.

Action Plan 47: Choices with Anger Model

Feelings of anger emerge in response to a trigger or activating event and at that point we may have options in how we respond. The choices we make will determine the outcome and any consequences.

Write down an anger 'trigger event', then consider a 'reaction' response or a 'let it go' response, with consequences for each. You decide which is appropriate in the moment for the event.

For instance, if the trigger is a road rage incident, we could choose to REACT by chasing after the driver, blasting the car horn, scream and shout with a possible consequence which might lead to violence or injury.

Or, we consider a LET IT GO response because it really isn't worth it, it's not worth upsetting ourselves unnecessarily, there's no real harm done, or the other driver might just be inexperienced or an idiot, or both. The consequence of letting it go, will be to de-escalate the situation.

Trigger event	React option?	Consequence	Let it go option?	Consequence	Preferred response
Example: Road Rage	Chase driver	Violence/injury	Not worth it	De-escalate	Not worth it

48

Developing Self-confidence

Spotlight

Self-confidence is a construct which is going to be different and unique for each of us. Someone who appears to be full of self-confidence might be quite different in reality. We can build up simple and effective masks which delude even the most seasoned observer into a clear mask of calmness, assuredness and self-confidence. Like a serene duck on the surface, we may be paddling our legs at a hundred miles an hour below the surface. Perception is a reality.

Self-confidence involves a self-awareness or personal assuredness of our skills, aptitudes, capabilities, competencies, judgements, abilities and qualities. Only we can define and determine our own self-confidence. It doesn't come from anyone else, though we can receive reassurance and confirmation to support our self-belief.

Ultimately, it's a state we can create about what we think or feel about ourselves. It involves a confidence we have in ourselves. If we enhance self-confidence by the experiences of mastering or completing tasks, then the secret lies in how we approach and carry out our tasks. They need to be achievable but they probably also need to stretch us a little bit each time, so we learn something new and develop greater knowledge and further skills.

Self-confidence is a crucial component of resilience because it creates a forward motion of positivity and optimism. Someone who is self-confident (and resilient) is likely to savour and relish challenges. They will face up to problems and difficulties and draw on their experiences and current capabilities to find a way to manage a situation, explore opportunities for change or seek out a solution.

Another essential ingredient involves being able to like oneself, even love oneself. This isn't selfish, egotistical or narcissistic. If we can't love ourselves and know what this means and how we achieve it, how can we possibly love someone else? What do we like about ourselves, what makes us proud of our achievements, chuckle at our humour, impressed by our resourcefulness, delighted by our creativity, marvel at our determination, savour our commitment, applaud our triumphs and so on?

There's trust in self-confidence too. Imagine the rope-walker high above us, a balancing pole helping to guide and support but underneath it's their self-confidence and mastery of the skill which will allow them to walk the rope. It's about an inner belief that we 'can do it'. We've done it before and we know we are capable. We need to have faith in what we know we can do.

Self-confidence doesn't make us perfectionists, quite the opposite. Self-confidence makes us realists, where we know what our reality is and our overall belief in what we know we can achieve. We don't delude ourselves about lofty ambitions, for there's no evidence of anything other than what we believe we can achieve.

Self-confidence involves self-understanding; we know what we can achieve as much as we know our limitations. We appreciate our continuum of capabilities and can adapt and change to meet new challenges and opportunities. We know we're not perfect and that there will be tough times when we might be tested beyond what we are prepared for. Drawing on our inner self-confidence resource will allow us to meet such challenges and thereby boost our self-confidence further.

Top Tips

Marvellous you

What can you applaud in you? Indulge in routine positive affirmations where you make time to appreciate who you are and what you're about, what you have learned and the successes you achieved. Similarly, reflect on how you have overcome obstacles. You are amazing. Believe it.

Face your fears

How do you deal with challenges and what influences your self-confidence? Deal with your issues head on. Bring in control and focus to become an architect of your solution, rather than being subservient to fate.

Who are you?

Create a map of your personality, identity and persona; who do you think you are? Then get significant others to do the same. Does anything differ in these perceptions and why? Reinforce the mutually identified positive traits and work on getting rid of the ones that disempower and serve no positive benefit.

Body talks

If you physically slouch or stoop, then psychologically you'll slouch and stoop. Irrespective of your height, stand up tall and proud, hold your head high, your shoulders back slightly; adopt an air of confidence and it will transcend over you. Become aware of your body language and whether is it closed or open; eye contact, how you smile, the tone of your voice and the speed at which you speak, your posture and how you hold yourself.

Random acts of kindness

Helping others will give you a feel-good boost which will enhance your positive self-worth. The more spontaneous and unplanned your worthy acts are, the more you will reap the intrinsic rewards.

Moral compass

Identifying your beliefs, value and morals will shape the person you are and aspire to be. By living your life under your defined code, you will support and enhance your sense of self. This may include connecting with a faith, religion or spirituality, but you can be moral without them.

Learning

Self-confidence can be bolstered through learning and developing, so you acquire more skills and competencies which in themselves widen your capacity to deal with issues, build greater insight and provide you with enhanced knowledge and wisdom.

De-clutter

There is much unnecessary clutter which exists in our lives; things we needlessly worry about and become preoccupied by. What meaningless and unhelpful clutter can you dispense with?

Silence negativity

If you have a persistent inner critic lambasting you all the time, fight it with a new positive voice which seeks to challenge your negativity. Seek out the evidence for your negativity and pessimism. Does your evidence reflect and justify the reality? Find the reasons behind this critical voice. A therapist or coach might help you identify, manage and turn the volume dial down on this unhelpful voice.

Action Plan 48: Self-confidence Scaling Plan

If self-confidence is an ongoing journey of learning to embrace new opportunities and possibilities, then enhancing your self-confidence comes from understanding how you develop, act and evolve.

The purpose of this exercise is to help you identify how you define your own self-confidence.

1. Map out a period of time; it could be a week, two weeks, a month.

2. Identify and keep a written log of your tasks and activities ahead.

3. Before each task, rate yourself from 0 to 10 in how self-confident you feel, with 0 = no self-confidence and 10 = maximum self-confidence.

4. Re-rate yourself after you have completed your task, using the same scale.

5. Has your self-confidence increased or decreased?

6. If it has increased, ask yourself how and why.

7. If it has decreased, what has happened and why?

8. Assess your 'before' and 'after' responses over your allotted period of time.

9. What changes do you need to adopt, how and why?

10. What can you learn from this and how can you nurture your self-confidence further?

49

Setting Meaningful Goals

Spotlight

The ability to create and meet goals is a useful way of building up our resilience. It's about getting things planned, then getting the jobs done. Without this, we can grind to a halt in a frenzy of inertia. Call them goals, aims or objectives they represent specific tasks which we set out to complete and achieve.

However, ineffective goal-setting not only contributes to stress and distress, but can also become a script for learned and persistent self-destructive behaviour, as we subconsciously deny ourselves the successes and achievements we deserve.

Learning a few tips about effective goal-setting can contribute significantly to resilience and sound personal self-management. We can learn to work with our aims and objectives so they become part of our identity and persona.

Goals are in some ways thoughts or cognitions as they indicate what our intentions are. However, in order to make them meaningful, we need to translate them from intentions to behaviours or actions. This could be a specific task, such as completing a nominated project by a set time.

All goals have some form of inspirational or motivational component to them in that they resonate value, meaning or importance to the individual. Without this, they remain disconnected and unconnected to the individual. There is an inherent learning component to goals, where they push us to a new place uninhabited before.

We don't find goals in the past; goals are almost always rooted in the future although they can start from the present and may link to the past. This makes goals aspirational; we aspire for something to happen and we commit and engage to achieve this.

There can be an unpredictability about goals, in that they don't necessarily deliver a fixed, clear or predetermined outcome. That would be more of a strategic plan or a strategy mapped out in detail from A to Z.

All goals have some flexibility and ambiguity, which makes them more intrinsically exciting and alluring. There's always some unknown quality and this is where the appeal lies. It provides leverage for creative dexterity, as we muster all the tools and skills to reach that goal.

Goals keep us sharp, in trim and up-to-speed. They test us and challenge us. But, perhaps, above all, they fuel ambition, which in turn ignites determination, desire, initiative, eagerness, enthusiasm, drive and a whole host of other positive attributes … all of which feeds into the tasty vegetable soup of resilience.

Top Tips

Be specific

Clarify as closely as you can, exactly what is required of your goal and why. You need to believe in it and create buy-in for yourself and others, so the detail is important. Too much ambiguity at this stage loses confidence and clarity and will lead to a vague, vacuous outcome.

Measure it

The point of measuring is so that you know where you are starting from and where you would like to end up. If you don't know where your start is, you'll certainly miss your target.

Is it achievable?

Many goals fall flat because they are unrealistic, over-ambitious or inappropriate. There needs to be some concept of the goal being achievable and possible. This is where you will be inspired to reach the end point. But you have to be open and honest about the achievability first. If you know you will get there, you will. If there's a lot of doubt, then it's less likely.

Resources in place

Goals don't work if you haven't got the correct resources in place. Do you have the skills, tools or people in place? Will these be sufficient for the duration of the task, or beyond?

On time

Can you complete the goal in time, especially if you are juggling other tasks at the same time? You need to give time to prepare, to act and to debrief or review. If you have to rush it, you may miss the opportunity to complete it in the best way possible. Similarly, if you give too much time, you may relegate the importance and do it a dis-service.

Engagement

There are many tasks we might complete on our own and indeed a goal is a construct which remains personal to us. But there are few goals which do not impact others in some shape or form. You might find the goal is bolstered by the support from or delegation to others. Publicly committing to a goal can increase your motivation and success in achieving it.

Reward yourself

Enjoy the journey working through the goal. The ultimate achievement is celebrated at the conclusion of the goal. You have now reached a point which deserves rightful praise and applause. The mere act of marking and rewarding yourself also serves as a future motivator for future goals.

Opportunity

To really inspire, you need to see the potential new achievement. Where and what are the new opportunities for you? Is it learning, outcome, collaboration, insight and so on?

Novelty

What is new in your goal which adds some uniqueness or sense that it is special and meaningful? If it has been all done before, it reduces the value of the outcome.

Economy

Can you achieve your goal in the most economical way, either time or resource-wise?

Action Plan 49: How to Achieve Goal SUCCESS?

Use the **SUCCESS** acronym systematically to help you achieve your goals.

Start from the beginning. What's your base or starting line?

_____

Understand where you are going. What's your outcome objective?

_____

Check you have resources to achieve the goal. What are your resource needs?

_____

Clarify the time required. When will you start, progress through and complete your goal?

_____

Ensure you have engagement of stakeholders. Who will best contribute to your goal?

_____

Shift the mindset to goal-achievement. What do you need to give you focus and drive?

_____

Savour the endpoint. Applaud completion, then audit, review and learn for the next time.

_____

50

Mindfulness

Spotlight

We spend so much of our lives ruminating, chewing over things that have happened, worrying about what we've said or done, or wired with anxiety about things we didn't say or didn't do. The past remains the past and fixed in history, yet it doesn't stop us brooding. But why does the past mean so much to us when we can't really do anything about it? It has happened, it has passed and it is over.

If the past is not troublesome enough, the same thing happens about the future—similar, but different worries, anxieties, concerns, fears, threats, uncertainties and doubts. And yet the future hasn't happened yet. It's in the future. We worry needlessly and endlessly and for what purpose?

It's amazing with the average amount of worry-time we give to the past AND the future, that we have any time left to live in the present. This is where the opportunity to be mindful emerges.

There's been a lot of interest in mindfulness of late, making it seem like the new big thing in stress management and resilience yet it owes much of its origins to Buddhist teachings as a way to develop self-knowledge and wisdom. Essentially, it's about the practice of conscious awareness, meaning that to be mindful, we need to bring our focused attention to something specific in our consciousness or active reality.

It also involves suspending judgement and opinion and observing an in-the-moment experience. This links to Person-Centred theory with empathic awareness (shared understanding), congruence (being true and real) together with an unconditional positive regard (being non-judgemental). Furthermore, mindfulness focuses on a way of being, which similarly parallels with the philosophy behind Person-Centred theory.

Some people are put off mindfulness as they believe it to be some obscure cult or that it's about sitting cross-legged and humming to a meditation trance. It's not about that and has been developed to be non-religious. Even the action plan is so simple you'll wonder why everyone's not practising it.

Anyone can do it, of any age, stature, affluence and fitness. It doesn't matter if you worry about the past, present and future, it's an antidote to all three time zones. And by adopting a few simple techniques, it's a positive mind and body ritual which can significantly contribute to help manage stress, anxiety, pain and depression.

It can be a challenge for those of us who are always wired and switched on to a relentless, quick and fired-up pace and firmly rooted to the rat-race conveyor-belt. This 'always-on-the-go' attitude might motivate, inspire and enthuse us, but we can often miss the small and beautiful things in life which we just pass on by without knowledge or awareness.

Mindfulness involves the conscious awareness of our thoughts, feelings and bodily sensations in relation to everything in the world around us with which we have contact. It's a positive grounding practice where we can connect and root ourselves 'in the moment' in a way that embellishes and enriches our experiences. We can see, feel, touch, smell, hear and be aware of things which might normally pass us by. And through this full-bodily awareness, it can feel like an active participation in, and connection between body, mind and spirit.

Top Tips

Worries of the past
What do you routinely worry about from the past, the things you cannot seem to shift, that lurk in your consciousness yet scurry about with no meaningful purpose? Name them. They have no role or purpose here. But do acknowledge that there may be issues from the past that can preoccupy your thoughts. Act on them, do something, seek closure, cleanse your mind.

Temper the future
Why worry about things in the future when they haven't happened yet. If you are anxious about something, deconstruct and identify the source of the anxiety and take some control over it. What benefit does the anxiety serve? Is your worry accurate? Stay in the present.

Breathe and focus
Normal breathing might be involuntary, but mindful breathing involves a focused, controlled and absorbing inhalation and slow, methodical exhalation. Recognise, feel and connect with your inhalation and your exhalation. Feel part of your breathing.

Body talks
As you become aware of your breathing and the capacity to slow and modulate it, focus on how your body feels. Do you feel heavy and drained, or energised, warm and uplifted? Generate awareness of all of your body, so your breathing and body connects together in symbiotic harmony.

Release the tension
With sustained breathing focus and an awareness of your body, become aware of pressure, stresses or tensions emanating from your body. Consciously release these pressures, let them free, allow them to leave your body, so you are left with your mindful breathing and body awareness.

Environment
With your enhanced self-awareness, use your felt-experience to resonate with the world around you; in your office room, as you com-

mute to work, when you convene with nature, in whatever space you inhabit. Absorb the environment around you and how you blend seamlessly within it.

Deafening silence

Noise is all around us, though we seem to tune out on demand. But find a time and a place to embrace silence. You might find silence eerie because you're not used to it. With silence comes an oasis of peace and a tranquillity of calm.

Thoughts floating away

You might find it difficult to 'stay in the moment' without thoughts and worries punctuating your mind. But that's OK. Just acknowledge them and let them float away as you focus on your breathing, your body and your environment. A thought is just a thought. You can replace one with another.

Practice

The more often you apply the principles of mindfulness, the easier it will become. Like riding a bike, you may grasp the basics as relatively simple, but you'll still be a bit wobbly until you get into a positive habit and build up your confidence and commitment.

Do nothing

The art or skill of mindfulness is not trying to master any specific intellect or faith or behaviour, but it's about slowing down the clock as you suspend time. Stop 'doing' and start 'being'.

Action Plan 50: 'Senses Working Overtime' Mindfulness[1]

Mindful breathing is an individual focus, because our bodies settle into a relaxed breathing rate which suits our body size and athleticism. Find a rate which suits you ... breathing in through your nose ... pause ... then slowly out through the mouth.

---

[1] With thanks to Sha'yo Lai (Counsellor) for reflections on this Action Plan.

Become aware of your body and your surroundings, then bring in your senses.

VISION

What do you see in front of you and to the side; the colours, the shapes, the fabric, the contrasts with other items next to it? What does colour say and mean to you? Do some colours feed your inner peace?

SOUND

What do you hear? Not just the background hum, but all the hundreds of sounds which make up the cacophony of noise; birds, the creak of a floor, a clock ticking, a siren in the background, the whirl of a computer fan, the distant sounds of footsteps, the hum of a plane overhead and so on.

TOUCH

What do you feel by your body or touch with your fingers? What does anything feel like; rough or smooth, abrasive or polished? How do you experience sensation and sensitivity? What is warmth like, or coolness?

SCENT

As you inhale through your nose, what can you smell? Can you name the smells, and if not, what are they similar to or remind you of? Can you notice the change in smells as you shift from one place to another? What do you notice most about these changes?

TASTE

When you eat your next meal, savour the flavour. What do your taste buds tell about foods and combinations of ingredients? Are there some which work well together and others which don't? Rather than just munching something small enough to swallow and move to the next mouthful, stay with one mouthful, chew slowly and think of what you're doing; let your taste receptors come alive.

51

Life Cycle Events: Losses and Gains

Spotlight

A central core of resilience is about developing the skills, harnessing the experiences and nurturing the competencies to manage a host of different situations which life will throw at us. Within all this, there is an expectation, even an anticipation, that things in life change and happen. Some may be within our control but much won't. Call it fate, circumstance, good luck or bad luck.

Change is a constant. We're always evolving, things happen, we adapt and we change. Consider your life trajectory to date. You may have your earliest memories involving scampering around on all fours, or dribbling in joy as you played with toys in your pram or in a crèche. And things changed. You maybe went to nursery, then primary or elementary school, then secondary or high school, perhaps got a part-time job, got into relationships, perhaps even broke up a few relationships, then college or university, then jobs, maybe new relationships, got a dog or a cat, married someone, brought a child into the world, moved home, sold the dog or it died, had more children, divorced and remarried, suffered bereavements and losses and so on.

You can start to read your own life story. It's packed with drama; the good and the bad, the joyful and the sad. We celebrate and mark the happy events, the successes and the achievements. And rightly so. That's about maintaining a sound positivity, embracing the good times when they roll in.

But resilience is not just about enjoying the good. It's about appreciating the wider picture and developing a context surrounding all of life. We revel in the good precisely because it provides a balance to the difficult events. Humans can't experience true happiness if they haven't experienced true sadness. One gives the other perspective.

Whilst this book champions positivity, it also champions realism. In the context of life events, it's nourishing for our resilience to recognise that many life events which seem to herald a positive change also mask a loss of some sorts. This is not to inject negativity just for the sake of it, but it's important as we develop resilience, to build a full picture. By doing so, we retain realism. We can still appreciate the good times. But perhaps, when the dust has settled, it is prudent to reflect on the potential losses peppered around the fringes of the positive changes.

A loss is not necessarily a negative thing. In this context, it's about recognising we might lose something when we gain something else. We can mourn the loss, if appropriate, or simply reflect on it. Doing so allows us to mark, acknowledge or appreciate the point of the change.

When we are young, we spent our time trying to look, appear or behave older than we are. Then a switch happens and we spend the rest of our lives trying to look and feel younger than we are. With the transition into adulthood, we gain this sense of maturity but we also lose our youth. If we have a happy childhood, perhaps we sometimes reflect back on a 'carefree youth', free from all the responsibilities of adulthood. If we had an unhappy childhood, then perhaps we look to create a more positive life where there is less suffering or angst.

With a new job promotion, we might celebrate success and achievement, maybe more income and greater recognition, but we also lose a previous work persona and change work relationships. Getting married heralds a union of two people into a future together, but we might lose a degree of prior independence. Similarly, having children offers an amazing new life change, but a potential loss of freedom and our own space and time.

We might consider some of these losses as inconsequential because of the gains involved, but life is about marking all the changes, all of the life events and the ups and downs, the losses and gains along the way. In this way we mark all of our experiences, rather than ignoring or suppressing the tough times or losses until they come back to haunt us later.

Accepting and appreciating the losses attributed to positive changes actually helps us to cope with bigger losses and more impactful tough life events in the future. This is part of developing a resilience to build our flexible coat of armour, to soften the blows of any future onslaughts.

Top Tips

Celebrate the good

To maintain positivity, seek out, mark and appreciate the worthwhile life events, changes and situations which warrant celebrating! Revel in the moment and enjoy the good that you deserve, appreciate your achievements and savour your successes.

Mark the losses

Consider the losses that emerge from positive changes. Acknowledge what has shifted and what you may be leaving behind. This will help you to move on with consideration and maturity. Life is not one long party. The party has to come to an end sometime. But we can look forward to, prepare for and enjoy the next party when it emerges.

Change has two sides

Any life cycle event forges a new perspective from a previous one. This is all part of life's rich tapestry; merging, shaping and meshing life situations from one to the next. Change can be exhilarating; it can also be daunting, breeding anxious anticipation and nervous excitement.

Deny denial

If you get married and swim along with the tide of coupledom without marking the loss of your single life, you may hit a stage when you suddenly miss that prior independence. But having appreciated the loss of that singledom independence, you can learn to embrace it when you are together, finding ways to maintain whatever independence and interdependence suits you both.

Accept change

Each life cycle event brings about some change with some positives and some potential losses. Being able to accept the reality of the change and how it shifts your perspective will allow you to settle in your new situation.

Frequency of changes

We often find that big changes happen in sequence and often without any real planning on our part. It's like you wait for a bus for ages, then three come at once. We can't control what those buses are doing, but we can control how we respond to them. Similarly, each life event needs dealing with one at a time so we can sufficiently process the impact on us and how we emerge from them.

Transformational growth

By accepting potential losses associated with positive life events, we can sometimes appreciate the meaning, value, growth or light which emerges from the apparent darkness. Humans are very adaptable, even if we feel we are not. We evolve and develop, and usually in spite of or because of life events. We learn, mature and bolster our resilience. We become stronger, we grow.

Action Plan 51: Life Cycle Event Balance

A natural river does not flow in a straight line. Neither does the trajectory of our life. The deviations evolve due to changes in rock formation, water flow, erosion and many other variables, like the external variables which we do not control in life.

Take yourself back to playing on a see-saw when you were a child; you were on one side and someone else was on the other. If you were perfectly balanced and still, the see-saw would not move. But an unequal weight imbalance or movement would have shifted the balance, sending you up and down.

Consider a recent life cycle event, and draw up the losses and gains in two columns. It's not to regard the losses as negatives and gains as positives, but to gain a perspective upon which you can reflect, mark, mourn (if necessary), learn from, celebrate and transformationally grow.

Life event: _____

Loss	Gain	Learning/Meaning/Growth
_____	_____	_____
_____	_____	_____
_____	_____	_____
_____	_____	_____
_____	_____	_____
_____	_____	_____
_____	_____	_____
_____	_____	_____
_____	_____	_____
_____	_____	_____

52

Rest and Relaxation

Spotlight

We live in a fast-paced society, everything whizzing past, people, noise, the constant message alerts on our mobile phones, social media, TV and so on. It's a stimulation explosion.

When do we actually experience peace and quiet, take a real break, enjoy tranquillity and silence? Probably not very often. In fact, many people say they hate silence; it's a void which has to be filled; the silence is deafening. That's because it's pretty alien to us. We don't know what to do.

Many of us may relax after a long day at work by putting our feet up and watching TV or as it seems to be these days, half watching TV and half tapping away into our mobile phone or tablet device. Distraction, distraction, distraction.

Even watching TV is a feast of visual and auditory stimulation; vibrant colours flashing in front of us or thumping music blaring out. We want to be entertained, to laugh or to experience drama or horror. It's still stimulation overload.

We're taught a host of academic subjects at school and we might learn to play sports and games but we're not usually taught how to rest and relax. It's as if this is not important, like we have an instinctive method for achieving this. But we don't.

We need to de-clutter our minds, to cleanse, purify and empty all the junk that fills up our headspace. And we need this because otherwise we just get more and more clogged up. We can reach saturation point and we can feel like we're going to explode. There's just too much going on. We worry about one thing or another, we're juggling work and home lives, and we get distracted by things that really don't impact on our world.

Consider the last time you watched or listened to a news programme. How much really impacted on you, your life or those nearest and dearest to you? Sure, news may be scary, sad or tragic but it fills our brains with more fears and worries. And it doesn't go anywhere.

We need to find that calm space; that place which grounds us and gives us a psychological break and an emotional holiday. We need to breathe out all the litter in our lives so that we can cleanse and nurture our body, mind and spirit. And then, we can get back out there into stimulation overdrive and cope better with the fast pace of life again. We might not be able to hide from or insulate ourselves from the acceleration of life, but we can learn to recharge, regroup and recuperate.

This will help us become more resilient. The greater resources we can employ to fight pressures and stresses, the more we can mitigate any negative impact or consequences. If you think of a waste bin; it gets filled with trash and soon it'll be full with no more room for anymore junk.

Our brains work in a similar way; we need to empty the waste so that we create a stimulation reservoir which now has the capacity to take on the rigours of life again.

Top Tips

Self-care

How do you look after yourself? Do you recognise when anxiety is starting to build up or you're getting progressively stressed? Spot the signs and you can do something about it. Take your foot off the gas and slow down. You'll thank yourself for it later.

Sleep hygiene

How much sleep do you need or get? Avoid stimulation drinks, such as with caffeine, at night. Resist alcohol as this can affect sleep. Stay off mobile phones and tablets two hours before bed. Try a warm herbal or milky drink before bed. If you have worries on your mind which might prevent you getting to sleep, write them down as this can help you discharge them from brain to paper.

Exercise

Rest and relaxation also includes getting enough exercise, which, in turn, can also improve sleep. Check out what exercise is appropriate for you; see your doctor if you need clarification and reassurance. Lack of exercise can contribute to lethargy and sluggishness.

Balanced diet

Getting the right nutritional diet can help your body to replenish and repair itself. Check out your salt, sugar and calorie intake, avoiding processed foods, which have limited nutritional value.

De-stress

We can all experience times of stress but to prevent this having a long term impact, identify what the sources of stress are and do something about it. Even small steps can make a big difference.

Anxiety

What do you worry about? Can you do something about it? If yes, then great, why worry? If you can't do anything about it, why worry?

Breathing

Whilst we breathe involuntarily, sometimes it can help to focus on and attend to our breathing. It's about slowing the pace of our breathing so we absorb more oxygen into our blood and help to reduce our heart rate. Feel the difference when you take a few long slow breaths.

Fun

We all need fun, enjoyment and laughter. This is important for relaxation. It can be a distraction from other demands as we focus on the moment. We're not worried about a work project when we're having a laugh. But get a balance. Seeking entertainment all the time will lose its impact.

Routine R&R

Build into your daily schedule a time when you rest, relax and unwind.

By making this a regular slot, you'll develop a positive habit which will help you to enjoy the calm down and help you prepare for the rigours of the next day.

Action Plan 52: Guided Visualisation for Relaxation

Lie or sit down in a comfortable, quiet, warm place. Close your eyes. Listen to the silence.

Breathe in through your nose, counting to four seconds, hold for four, then slowly exhale through your mouth for four seconds. Repeat this throughout this exercise.

Picture a scene with which you are familiar and which gives you a happy, relaxed feeling, like a beach, a walk along a countryside track or next to a gentle meandering stream. In this example, we'll use the stream.

What do you see? The sun high above the hills flicking down onto the trickles of water. What colours do you see? Are the trees waving in the distance, grasses dancing in the fore-ground? Maybe some wildlife; birds soaring above, or darting at the edge of the stream. Are there fish jumping? Maybe a deer or rabbit in the distance eating contentedly.

What do you hear? The trickle of water, the chirping of the birds, the waft of wind, the buzz of bees?

What can you smell? The clean, fresh air, as you breathe in the scene. The smell of trees and vegetation, the smell of the earth, the scent of the land.

What do you feel? The warmth of the sun on your face, the flick of a breath of wind, the earth beneath your feet, the sure-footed path on which you walk.

What do you taste? You have a sit down to savour your special place, with a cool refreshing drink as you munch on a favourite healthy sandwich, taking in all the flavours and tastes.

This is your safe place, a place where you can examine all the tensions and stresses in your life. Look at your tensions and stress.

Imagine them as having a shape and colour. Look at their size. Look at them carefully. Look at their shape. Look at their colour. As you see your tension and stress take shape, you will notice that slowly they begin to move away from you. They no longer trouble you. You are free of all tension and stress.

Focus on this wonderful safe place, and absorb what you can sense around you so you continue to feel relaxed and stress free.

Focus on your breathing, in for four, hold for four, out for four.

When you feel rested and relaxed, open your eyes and smile.

53

Looking After Yourself and Self-Care

Spotlight

We spend a lot of time looking after other people, whether this is a child, an elderly parent or relative, someone at work who needs support or a friend in need. In some ways it's easier to take care of other people. We might get a feel-good factor knowing that we are very much appreciated for our efforts. And helping others does make us feel good, undoubtedly.

But what about us? Who looks after us? Do we look after us? We're not so good at that. We're not taught at school how to look after ourselves. Perhaps society focuses on how we need to help others, and this might start from school age, as we join clubs and societies or religious groups and scouting or guiding associations all intent on helping others and of being of service to others. Obviously this is good for society and there's nothing wrong with this but we can lose sight of our own needs along the way.

We ignore the fact that we need to look after ourselves. It can feel a bit of an alien concept to develop a focus, plan or strategy of self-care, but why not? If we're in a mess, we're not going to be much good to others, including within our families or at work. Maybe there's a role and purpose for us to focus on what our needs might be and the self-nurturing required of ourselves. It's not selfish; it's about taking responsibility to and for ourselves. We owe it to ourselves.

And yet we can feel it's a guilty pleasure to indulge or treat ourselves, as if it's wrong. But why is it wrong? Maybe it's not familiar to us and that in itself is a significant sign of omission and self-neglect. What's wrong with indulging ourselves, of appreciating and applauding ourselves, of feeling proud and content, happy and joyful? We all have needs and meeting some of these needs can be integral to looking after ourselves.

If we feel overloaded or stressed, taking time out and having a break is an act of self-care. We might work hard and over long hours, but having a weekend off or taking a holiday is an act of self-care. It might be a regular self-appreciation and positive focus for ourselves or it could be in relation to setbacks and disappointments; we might feel deflated after not getting the promotion we sought, so going out and buying something nice for ourselves as a 'pick-me-up' is an act of self-care (keeping it in proportion, of course).

Eating healthily is good for us and necessary for the body to operate optimally. Food helps to energise and nourish our bodies. It can also be fun and make us feel positive. Preparing a meal takes effort yet it reinforces the time we are giving ourselves for sustenance, nurturing and self-appreciation.

Self-care is an important ingredient of resilience where we assert our right for positive self-worth and self-confidence together with a willingness to value and appreciate ourselves. We might value and appreciate our motor car (or other cherished object); so we might moderate excessive and harsh driving, keep it serviced and well maintained, polish and clean it but do we do the same for us, at least in a methodical and conscientious way? Our motor might be doing well at our expense. Can we learn from how we treat our vehicle? Hopefully we're going to last a lot longer than it, yet do we invest comparable care in us?

Most often, probably not.

Top Tips

How do you help others?

Recognise how, why and when you help other people. Turn the focus round on you and what you can identify as the opportunity to pay closer attention to your help requirements. Use what you do for others as a model or guide for caring for yourself.

What are your needs?

What are the things that you need in life which offer you safety and security, nourishment and fulfilment, satisfaction and contentment? Differentiate between your 'needs' and your 'wants'. Focus on your needs and you may find that your wants change.

You're worth it

Create a daily mantra that reinforces a commitment to your self-worth. Feed into it daily and challenge any misconception about you NOT being worth it. If you find a challenge to this, explore what the barriers or blocks might be. Speak to a therapist if this helps you enhance your self-worth.

Take a break

Step back from the rat race and rigours of your daily life and pause for thought and contemplation. The world's not going to stop if you do, so you can step back onto the conveyor belt of life soon, but do take a break when you can so you can recharge your batteries.

Work-life balance

Assess how you can achieve a better and more consistent balance to your lives at work and home. Add to your life enjoyable non-work related stuff and you may feel more energised when you return to work. This might seem counterintuitive but it happens.

Live for you

Do you live your life at home or work because it's what you believe other people want? What do you want? How might you be different if you lived your life around what's important for you?

Healthy lifestyle

You deserve it to yourself to enjoy and benefit from regular exercise, a nutritious diet, a good sleep every night and healthy and nurturing life-style behaviours. You don't deserve to be unfit, lacking of motivation, tired and unhealthy.

The social

Humans are social creatures, and this includes you, even if you get back from work exhausted and don't want to see or talk to someone. But you do need the social interaction of family and friends. Build in time for this. You might feel you can't be bothered or it's an effort, but you'll usually appreciate the effort made to be social. Mix it with a hobby or sport and you'll create a greater inclination to commit.

Interests

What are all the things you have enjoyed in the past or have an interest in trying out in the future? Sports, activities, interests, pursuits, hobbies, volunteering, clubs and societies, associations and so on? Engage with whatever provides you with enthusiasm, but not where this takes over or becomes excessive or counterproductive. Get a balance which sustains your enjoyment.

Action Plan 53: Self-Care 'Feel-Good' Checklist

Read the following statements about self-care.
Score '1' if the statement is true for you, or '0' if it is not.

- __ I look after myself physically and take care of my appearance.
- __ I take a break or rest when I feel tired, exhausted or stressed.
- __ I eat a balanced, nutritious diet and maintain my weight.
- __ I am aware of my emotional needs.
- __ I get sufficient sleep every night and wake up fresh and revitalised.
- __ I know how to cope with or get out of stressful situations.
- __ I engage in hobbies, activities, interests or pursuits.
- __ I give myself praise, appreciation and pride now and again.
- __ I engage with a social life which is right for me.
- __ I take time out to do things which I want to do.
- __ I can say 'NO' to others, when I need to say 'YES' to me.

― I do something which gives me contentment each and every day.
― I believe I am a good person.
― I give myself a well-deserved treat now and again.
― Other people would say I look after myself.
― I value and appreciate myself as much as I value and appreciate others.
― I get regular exercise and keep fit and healthy.

― ....
― ....
― ....

___ **Total score?**

Add three more of your own self-care 'feel-good' options.

Score 20, and you're in top form and really understand what self-care is about. Score under 10 and you need to make changes to your life and focus more on YOU.

54

Problem-Focused Resilience

Spotlight

We cope with struggles and crisis situations in a range of different ways, though we rarely adopt a logical, consistent approach. Sometimes we might need to adapt to circumstances, so one method of coping isn't always going to deliver the best solution. But introducing a repertoire of coping and resilience-focused styles gives us the choice to select a more appropriate one for the situation.

Problem-focused coping is about targeting or identifying the root cause of the problem. This is quite different to emotion-focused coping, which seeks to manage the emotional response or reaction to the issue. Whilst the former approach is suitable for stressors which can be changed or eliminated, the latter works with situations that cannot readily be changed, but where the emotional reaction can be. Each situation will determine the degree to which each can be adopted.

This chapter focuses on problem-focused coping because emotions management, discussed elsewhere, can be used as a comparable emotions-focused coping technique.

Problem-focused coping is a rationale, functional, information-oriented and facts-based approach. It centres on identifying the cause of the issue and trying to deal with the problem at that stage. This is similar in approach to a primary stress management intervention, in that a key aim is to find ways to get rid of the original stressor or the source of stress.

The premise is that eliminating the source of the stress gets rid of the reason to be stressed, and so when the stressor disappears, then any dysfunctional or impactful emotional reaction or negative-thinking response also goes with it.

It can be easy for a stressful situation to be exacerbated by emotions, which we call emotional hijacking. Similarly we can experience cognitive or psychological hijacking too, where our thinking gets out of hand or proportion, possibly by catastrophising or mis-cued thinking.

However, keeping the focus on emotions, we can feel swamped by them and unable to cope. We grasp reality by focusing on the facts and information.

For example, it's 10 am and my boss wants me to complete a business case for a new recruit in my team and submit this by close of play today. I panic, I need much longer than that, I fear if I don't do this I won't get the new recruit, or worse, it'll look bad on me, I won't get the promotion I seek, or I might even be demoted or fired, then I'll never get a job again and we'll have to downsize, take the kids out of school, sell the car ….

Facts—I have a tight deadline, need to prioritise and maybe delegate or ask for more time. Period.

All the rest is emotion and negative-thinking overload, which becomes the chief stress combo. It hijacks what might otherwise be sufficiently managed through a problem-focused strategy.

Top Tips

Step back
Take a slow breath in and a slow breath out. Pause for thought and consideration. Stand back from the issue or problem and build a perspective into the situation.

Movie magic
Imagine you're watching a CCTV feedback of you and your situation. What's going on that you don't readily see in the moment?

Take back control

Much stress can emerge from a fear of losing control or becoming paralysed and impotent because of this fear of losing control. What can you do to bring some control, authority or responsibility back into the situation?

Focus on the facts

Gather all the information and intelligence about the situation and, importantly, any relevant background information. What you see at face value may only be a small part of the overall picture.

All perspectives

You will have your perspective on the situation and how it impacts you, but what about others affected by the issue. Their perspective may offer a new insight in terms of your fact-finding exercise and/or offer some options for delegation, reconceptualisation of the issue or resolution.

Choices and options

As soon as you have at least one 'way out' or resolution, you have an option. Get another, and you have choices. Build on your choices and however wayward they might seem, some of the best solutions can come from an initially abstract and bizarre concept.

Empowerment

You start to respond to and resolve the stress situation when you empower yourself to do something about it. At this stage, it's about developing a logical, coherent and timely plan. You're basing your stress analysis on the facts of the source of stress. Apply the same strategic mindset to plot and plan your action.

Take action

And then you implement your action plan. What will you do, how and when? As soon as you act, you'll feel strength, control and empowerment flood back, to the effect that the stressor will start to recede and morph into something much more controllable and containable.

Delegate

You might not be able to do everything on your own. Who can help or assist? Split down tasks into bite-sized chunks and you can ask more people to chip in, so you get the synergistic benefits from team work and cooperation.

Negotiate change

If you can't resolve the problem, then what can you do to negotiate the way the problem emerged in the first place or the demands placed upon you? Can you negotiate a different meaning of the problem or stressor? Or can you negotiate a different desired outcome which mitigates the stress?

Action Plan 54: Problem-Focused 10-point Strategy

1. Name the issue and the facts surrounding it.

   _____

2. Identify any emotional or psychological hijacking which is distorting perspective.

   _____

3. What has caused the issue?

   _____

4. What might be an immediate solution, plus alternative solutions?

   _____

5. What control can you bring into the situation?

   _____

6. Who can help, support or aid you?

   _____

7. What is the ideal or preferred outcome?

   _____

8. Create a practical and realistic plan with time line and action points.

   _____

9. Implement your action plan.

   _____

10. Review and monitor progress and identify what learning can be gained from this experience.

    _____

55

Solution-Focused Resilience

Spotlight

A solution-focused approach is not simply the flip side of problem-focused coping; it is a fundamentally different model. Traditionally, we lean towards a problem focus, by fixating on what the problem is, what caused it and trying to get away from it, a sort of cause-consequence-cure approach. This means rooting ourselves in the original issue rather than the destination. In many cases this can, of course, be an effective self-management tool, so it is not to be disregarded or ignored.

However, solution-focused resilience is about orienting ourselves primarily into a forward, directional alignment with options, potential solutions or resolutions. It is goal and future focused and targets our strengths.

In most cases, if we have a problem and then focus on and achieve a desired solution, then the problem disappears and we have no need to revisit the problem. However, as with all effective stress management strategies, sometimes we need to understand the source or trigger of the problem, so we can minimise or negate a repeat of that problem in the future.

A problem focus tends to obsess around one's weaknesses and limitations, whereas a solution approach veers more into strengths and opportunities. It's using the resources we already have and expanding on them, rather than looking at the gaps which may need filling. In this way, it's often a quicker approach and one which can be applied to many different scenarios in rapid succession.

There are times when we all have to admit that we like a good moan. We like (perhaps need) to complain about something which has happened or vent our emotions. This can be an important way to express ourselves, to acknowledge a problem and to bring it into conscious awareness.

But if this becomes a habit, then it can become self-defeating and self-destructive, or just downright negative. And negativity can breed further negativity, until we're in a continual cyclone of negativism, which can further prompt low mood, apathy and depression.

Solution-focused resilience can be regarded as a philosophy or 'way of being'. We classify this as a resilience tool because it can be effective at dealing with difficult situations quickly and shields us from conflicts when they emerge. It also taps into existing coping skills and strategies so it can be readily accessed when required.

Practice it, breathe it, absorb it, integrate it, model it and adjust it to best suit you, your world and your philosophy and it will become a normal part of ongoing resilience for you.

Top Tips

Desired future

Based on Steve de Shazer's 'miracle question', if you woke tomorrow and your problem had disappeared, what would you be doing positively or how would your life have improved? How would you be living your life differently and how can you start doing this now?

Scale yourself

Using a scale of 0 (nowhere near it) to 10 (solution achieved), rate yourself regularly from your starting point, through your efforts to achieve the solution, to that final resolution point. Scaling helps you to assess where you begin, and the stages you master as you reach your goal.

Others to scale you

Do the same rating exercise but this time get others to evaluate where they scale you. Is this different to your score and if so why? Why have they scored you differently?

Past successes

Think of a similar problem or issue and consider how you have resolved this before. What did you learn and what tools or initiatives did you engage? Can you apply this or something similar now?

Avoid problems

OK, you might start with a problem, but leave it there. You're now oriented to dealing with the solution, how your future will be and what you'll be doing differently.

Resources audit

Consider the skills and tools you have at your disposal which you can utilise to achieve your solution. If you don't have them, identify someone who can help you who does.

Necessary steps

What needs to happen in order for you to get close to reaching your solution? Is this something you need to act on or does it relate to a state of mind or thinking?

Baby steps

Sometimes you might need to take small steps to reach your solution, so that you can consolidate and reinforce the change and improvements required. But this is not to stop you taking a decisive and positive leap if this works for you too.

Reward

When you have reached your solution point, or as close as you need to get, celebrate and applaud yourself so that you make this a positive reinforcement of your success and a model for the future.

Learning

What did you learn from this exercise and what can help you identify, and achieve new solutions in the future? What advice would you give to YOU for next time? Or what would you do differently?

Teach others

How would you coach others to replicate your Solution-Focused Resilience plan? Sometimes you can learn about yourself by how you might advise others. Can you practice what you preach?

Action Plan 55: Solution-Focused Time Machine

1. Identify your issue, difficulty or problem.

   _____

2. Imagine you are in a colourful, hi-tech time machine, with your finger pressed on the FAST-FORWARD button whizzing through time, and you suddenly screech to an abrupt stop when you reach your solution. What would your solution look like?

   _____

3. How would you know that THIS is THE solution?

   _____

4. What would be happening differently in your new world and to you?

   _____

5. Wind back your time machine by pressing the SLOW-REWIND button. From the future to your present, chart in reverse order all the different stages that you believe occurred from the future solution point right back to your original problem point.

___

6. Translate your journey to a reality when you can start to plan your solution.

___

7. Scale yourself to monitor and measure each stage of your progress to reach your solution.

___

8. Applaud your success and achievement when you reach your solution. And learn from it. What have you learnt?

___

56

Change-Focused Resilience

Spotlight

Bookshops are stuffed with business books dedicated to managing change on the premise that we don't naturally like change, we don't want it, and we struggle to cope with it. We prefer the status quo. We like to have familiarity so we know how the land lies and we can develop a structure or norm within which we do our work. It gives us a foundation.

Faced with change, we sometimes react and kick out. It takes us into an unfamiliar place, where we have to find a new equilibrium. It means we need to be more adaptable and tolerant of ambiguity as we clarify the boundary of the new norm. And one change often opens the door to another, with the expected knock-on effect of the consequences of change.

Change is the one constant in our lives. Organisations continually strive to improve processes or find better ways of doing things so they can remain competitive. Customer expectations change too, whether this relates to a product or to the service which is demanded. This requires companies to keep in tune with demand and meet, and exceed, what is sought.

Life at home can change too. Changes at work can impact on us at home, maybe altering our working hours or increasing the time demands on our workflow. Or family issues may trigger change; as children grow up and school or university demands require us to adapt to their needs, or how elderly relatives find their needs change or aspects to our relationships with partners and friends shift.

Nothing stays still for long and we can often find we are sailing on a sea of change, where we concentrate on staying afloat, finding a way to navigate the choppy waters. This might mean we are paddling fast and going nowhere fast too, just trying to keep our heads above water.

BUT, this chapter is about grabbing change as a crucial vehicle for coping. Rather than finding ways to minimise and mitigate change, we advocate seeking and embracing change. Often, stress emerges when things happen and we feel we have no control over what has happened or the consequences of it, or we have lost control and are floundering.

Similarly, we may experience moments of anxiety, panic, low mood or depressive feelings because we feel trapped with no apparent way out. We feel locked into a situation which destabilises or paralyses us and this inertia grinds us to a halt. Faced with the perception of this trappedness, we retreat (through depression), panic (anxiety and fear) or overreact (anger and aggression).

The antidote here is to explore change as both an option and the solution. By establishing a person-centred change strategy, that is finding a change which suits us, we regain some control.

The mere act of exploring change can also contribute to increased self-worth, increased self-confidence and increased self-belief, not to mention an increase in overall positivity and enhanced emotional well-being. This is because you're actually doing something, rather than doing nothing.

Top Tips

Keep it positive

Effective change needs to be positive in intention and outcome, that is, change for the better. It might be easy to change something because the option is there, but you need it to be the right change for you.

Baby steps

It's often more practical and achievable if you make smaller bite-sized changes, rather than big 'change of life' alternatives. 'Baby steps' allow you to pause for breath, assimilate the effects of the previous steps and use momentum to adapt your options or direction.

Knee jerk

Be wary of knee-jerk reactions. If you hate your boss or job, resigning your job is certainly an option, but is it the best change for you at this time?

Take time

Change might be appropriate, but just not at this time. You might achieve a better result if you delay change to a more appropriate or opportune time.

Feedback

Get help and support from others. What would others recommend or advise if you were to make the change you are considering. Sometimes it can be really helpful if you get feedback from the right people—you might be overlooking things which others could highlight.

Be SMARTER

Just like effective delegation of tasks and objectives, make your change SMARTER: Specific, Measureable, Achievable, Resourced, Timely (and you are) Engaged and Rewarded.

Delegate or nominate

It might be that someone else making a change will have a better impact or result than if you made the change. Ask around, explore who's involved and the capacity for them to help you here.

Mind your attitude

Consider how you have responded to change in the past. What is your approach, mindset or attitude to change? If you recoil in fear at change, you might find a self-created change strategy difficult though you might also find it enlightening and empowering.

Choices

Change gives us the potential to shift from one state to another. It gives us what opens up the world of choice. The more choices we can find, the less dramatic or threatening change can feel.

Consequences

Consider the consequences, short, medium and long term, if possible. This is not to paralyse you to make change where change is due but it's to encourage a considered assessment. Change in haste, repent at leisure.

Necessity

Do you really need to make the change you have considered? Maybe it's the thought of it? If we feel stuck, the prospect of change can appear very alluring and intoxicating. But is it right?

Change audit

When you make a considered change, review how it all went. Was it the right change to make at the right time? If so why? If not, why not? Did we have enough options? Did we have sufficient intelligence or information? Learning constructive lessons will enable us to be better equipped to make the most appropriate timely change in the future.

Action Plan 56: Change-Focused Coping Plan

This model is geared to the reader who feels emotionally or psychologically stuck or trapped.

If you need or want to change something, respond to the following questions.

1. How or why do you need to make the change?

2. What are the different change choices?

   _____

3. How have you determined the choices for the change you are considering?

   _____

4. Identify another five change options.

   1. _____

   2. _____

   3. _____

   4. _____

   5. _____

5. What is the Number One change choice and why?

   _____

6. What would your family or close friends say about your change choice?

   _____

7. What difference would it make to delay your change by days, weeks, years and so on?

   _____

8. Pick a famous person you admire; what would they say about your proposed change?

9. What are the consequences of making the change (to self, family, job, finances etc.)?

10. What would be the consequences for NOT making the change?

57

Managing a Crisis

Spotlight

Despite the best of intentions and careful planning, we cannot be totally prepared for everything. We might be doing a great job at work and suddenly find we are threatened with redundancy. Or we take out insurance for our cars or homes, hoping that we'll never actually need to make a claim. Or we suffer some physical accident at home or work, sport or recreation.

We think that things always happen to other people, but not us. Strangely, we feel immune to a crisis. We'll be OK. We'll nip under the crisis radar. Our luck will hold. But then … wham!

It's suddenly our turn. And it can turn our lives upside down, and especially as we did not ever think it would happen to us. That's why it hits us hard, as a crisis. We were not fully prepared. We did not think it would happen. But it does. And somehow we need to pick ourselves up and dig ourselves out of the hole.

A crisis by its definition is an unusual event which was unexpected. It's an abnormal event and so we react to it in a plethora of different ways, unaccustomed with knowing what we should or should not do, feel or think. It usually triggers a tornado of raw emotions, skewed thinking patterns and irrational behaviours. But they are all normal reactions to an abnormal event.

We are not immune to a crisis. We cannot be fully prepared for a crisis either. Terrible and traumatic events do happen in life. The media hooks us with one trauma after another, yet from the safety of a television, radio or PC, we feel some disconnection, buffer or insulation from reality.

A really significant crisis usually changes our lives in a way where it will never be the same again. The extent to which our lives will change is determined by how we bounce back from it to recover. The impact may be significant but the consequences can be mitigated and managed by how we choose to respond and deal with it.

In the depth of a crisis, the imperative is to survive and make sense of what is happening. We will be bewildered and paralysed. We will have tunnel thinking. We will be totally preoccupied. We may behave irrationally, spontaneously and without consideration. We might vent intense anger and frustration or we might cocoon ourselves in a blanket of depression or anxiety. All these are normal responses, even if we surprise or perplex ourselves with them.

Top Tips

Insurance

If you're reading this chapter and you haven't yet experienced a major crisis get adequate insurance! The whole point of insurance is you are insuring against a potential future loss. You can't predict if and when it might happen. Better to be insured and not to need it, rather than not be insured and need it.

It's not personal

A crisis can happen to anyone. If it happens to you, it's very unlikely to be your fault, it's nothing personal and it's probably just your bad luck.

Crisis inoculation

If you believe you are at more risk to a specific crisis than most people, because of where you live, or the job you do, it might make sense to make some provisional preparations for responding to or dealing with a crisis. In this way, preparedness offers a degree of insulation.

Response audit

After a crisis hits, review, reassess and reappraise how you are thinking, feeling and acting. It might surprise you how you are responding. Monitor how this changes and increases or reduces over time. It is not unusual to find oneself locked in a particular train of thought or emotion.

Mitigate consequences

In any crisis, you want to limit the damage or negative effect. What actions can you take now to mitigate the consequences and de-escalate the situation?

Dream team

Who are the key people you need around you to help you through this crisis? This could be family and friends, but maybe also your doctor, lawyer, insurance broker, financial advisor, therapist and coach?

Take stock

A crisis usually hits us hard, winding us emotionally and psychologically. But in the murky uncertainty and fallout, it can help to seek out a proper reality check of the situation. How are things, what has changed, what needs to change, and what is required to shift to some resolution?

Grounding

What provides you with psychological stability? What makes you feel safe emotionally? How do you ground yourself? Music, creativity, talking, relationships, exercise, healthy living and so on?

Transformational growth

Most people who have been through a life crisis report some transformational growth as a result. Something emerges which offers new meaning or changes how we see life, for the better. Green shoots of recovery peak through the ashes. An arrow needs to be pulled back on a bow before it can be catapulted forward. Sometimes, a few steps backwards can find a way of catapulting us forward, even if it doesn't make sense at the time.

Action Plan 57: A Bio-Psycho-Social Approach to Crisis Management

Recovery from a crisis involves effort and planning.

In the vast majority of cases, a crisis is exacerbated because of confusion, misinformation and a lack of clarity. The first golden rule of not making a drama out of a crisis is to gather as much facts as possible. You need to know solid, reliable information. What is happening, what has happened, what are the circumstances, who is involved, how is the situation changing, and what do you need to do to stay safe and secure?

Once you are in a position of clarity and safety, you can move to a more bio-psycho-social framework for recovery.

Assess the impact on your physical self (bio), psychology (psycho) and community (social).

Physical (bio) Review any physical injury or consequences (keep safe).

Monitor changes to diet, sleeping, drinking and exercise patterns.

Maintain a routine for sleeping and eating.

Psychological (psycho) Assess your thinking patterns and any negative thinking.

Reduce catastrophising by normalising your thinking.

Create a reality check on your wider environment or situation.

Normalise any anxiety and depression to being associated with the event.

Appreciate normal reactions to an abnormal event.

Community (social) Harness the support of friends and family.

Connect with your wider social environment (as available).

Talk to others, either associated with the event or not, as appropriate.

Keep in touch with those associated with the event.

Seek professional support as available.

58

Avoiding Burnout

Spotlight

Many of us might have seen someone on the brink of burnout but it's quite different when this is happening to us and difficult to see it creeping up on us.

We define burnout as exhaustion due to a combination of emotional, psychological and physical factors which are sustained and prolonged. It is the insidious accumulation of such problems which differentiates burnout from stress. Although not strictly a medical term, the signs and symptoms of burnout can be observed and might include a variety of impacts from the following clusters.

Psychologically, we may have difficulty concentrating or making rational decisions; our thinking could be increasingly negative, skewed or distorted and we might find ourselves forgetful or absent-minded. Generally, our capacity to cope with and manage issues will reduce as we lose the foresight and depth of thinking skills to mediate and mitigate the onslaught of tension and angst.

Emotionally, we may feel a tsunami of feelings bewildering and overwhelming us, peppered with high levels of anxiety and tension, demotivation and apathy, depression and sadness, low self-esteem and self-worth, moodiness and irritability, shame and guilt, and a misdirected and a misinterpreted imbalance of anger and aggression.

Physically, we might experience dysfunctional changes to sleep and an inability to relax, fluctuating eating habits and weight gain or loss, increasing tiredness and fatigue, accelerated breathing and heart rate, hot and cold sweats, a greater susceptibility to colds, viruses and flu, muscle aches and pains particularly round the neck and back, and a general feeling of malaise and exhaustion.

Behaviourally, we might find we're clutching to inappropriate mood enhancers, including, but not limited to, nicotine products, prescription and recreational drugs, plus alcohol. Or we could be maxing out on other 'positive' addictive behaviours such as gym exercise and running. We may be isolating ourselves or avoiding social or work situations or conversely we might be resisting and reacting to being alone.

Linked to all of this, a feeling of burnout can also trigger thoughts about wishing we could escape everything and not have to deal with it. Or more than this, wishing we were dead and feeling so overwhelmed with no apparent way out.

Burnout is often incremental. It can creep up on us. First we experience pressure, then pressure starts to merge into stress, then the stress just hangs on in there and before we know it we are feeling out of control without any semblance of how to step back and step out of the downward spiral.

By the time we're approaching burnout, it's likely that other people will have alerted us in their own way to their concerns about us. But most likely, we will have ignored them, misled them that we were OK, disbelieved them, glossed over the severity of the situation or explained that there's nothing we can do about it. Feelings of burnout or exhaustion might also mimic the signs of depression and acute anxiety.

There's always something we can do about it. The first step is to put our hands up and admit we're out of our depth and need help. The next step is to find help and reach out to accept it. In most cases, your doctor should be the first person you consult.

Top Tips

Work-life balance
Construct a time line over the week and check how much time you allocate for relationships, family, fun, rest and relaxation, hobbies or interests and 'me time'. If you can't find the time for this, make some changes so that you can.

Stress triggers
Take a step back and reflect on the different sources of stress for you; how do they emerge and why, and what can you do to deflect or manage them?

Rest and relaxation
We all need quality rest, to slow down, pause and breathe. Consciously consider what relaxation options work for you; TV, a movie, a meal with friends, a walk in the park, a swim, reading, music?

Moderate alcohol
Alcohol might seem to give you a release and relief especially if you are with friends during these times, but overindulgence creates the hangover which just adds to the doom and gloom and incapacity to cope. Your stresses may remain and you've just added low mood to the mix.

Delegate
If you feel overloaded and overwhelmed, who can help spread the load, at home and work?

Just say NO
Say 'NO' to more work and 'YES' to help, support, guidance, advice and collaboration.

Support network
Develop, maintain and make use of social support, family, relatives, old and new friends and external and independent resources. Try a coach, mentor or therapist, if this helps.

Change what you can

Do something specific and actionable, which shifts something difficult to a more positive place.

Accept what you can't change

There's no point pushing against something which you have no capacity to change. Accept any challenges or limitations and you'll find that an acceptance strategy lifts some pressure from your midst and allows you to move on.

Ventilate

Don't internalise your angst and frustration. Find a way to express and ventilate how you are feeling. Emotional intelligence involves appropriate expression of your core emotions. Express yourself.

One step at a time

Break down your stresses into manageable chunks and deal with one issue at a time, rather than all at once. Small bites of progress will escalate positivity and you'll feel you are moving forward.

Stay healthy

You will cope better with stress if you eat a balanced diet, exercise, maintain a sufficient sleep pattern and generally look after yourself, including personal hygiene (if you look bad, you'll feel bad).

Action Plan 58: A-B-C Burnout Checklist

The checklist below may help you identify the signs and symptoms of burnout.

Select the score which applies to you using the following five-point scale;

1. Never
2. Rarely
3. Sometimes
4. Most of the time
5. All of the time

Affective (Emotional)	Score (1–5)
A1. My emotions are out of control	__
A2. I feel extremely frustrated or angst	__
A3. I feel tearful or emotionally fragile	__
A4. I feel very anxious or agitated	__
A5. I experience low mood or depression	__
Behavioural (Actions)	
B1. I feel physically exhausted	__
B2. Work tasks are beyond my capacity to cope	__
B3. My appetite or sleep is affected	__
B4. I have headaches, migraine or back/neck pains	__
B5. I have difficulty relaxing or switching off	__
Cognitive (Thinking)	
C1. I cannot concentrate	__
C2. I have distorted or confused thinking	__
C3. I experience forgetfulness	__
C4. I have persistent, negative thoughts	__
C5. I have difficulty making decisions	__
Total score	____

Score 0–29	You may be experiencing a low to moderate risk of burnout.
Score 30–44	You may be experiencing a moderate to high risk of burnout.
Score 45–75	You may be experiencing a high risk of burnout.

Please Note

People experience and respond to stress differently. This subjective checklist does not constitute a medical diagnosis. If you have concerns about your physical or mental health, please consult with an appropriate medical professional.

59

How to Tolerate Ambiguity

Spotlight

Some of us have quite fixed views about how we see the world or how we think things should be. It's fine to have opinions and views. But sometimes having our fixed views may lead us into a situation where we are dealing with others who do not share our views. This can lead to conflict and disagreement. This is not to say you shouldn't be able to make up your own mind.

We shape our views, opinions and judgements throughout our life, influenced by a multitude of variables: the views of our parents, family, friends and work colleagues, upbringing and background, the influence of the media and especially social media, reactions to and response from others in the past, and how we have connected or disconnected with others in the past who both share or do not share our perspectives.

Developing our views is an important aspect of shaping our identity and personality. It contributes to defining who we are and what we're about, our loves and hates, our passions and dreads, all of which gives meaning, substance and belief to ourselves and the world in which we live.

A key component of resilience is having the capacity to adapt in the face of adversity. In fact, that's been the secret of successful evolution since time began. Think of the species that were land based but learnt to swim or aquatic creatures that learnt to fly or those which evolved to become faster, more agile, larger, more protected, better insulated, able to withstand immense heat or cold, or live in extreme and hostile environments.

OK, that's just animals, birds and fish … consider how humans have evolved, and in so doing, what we have learnt, created, inspired, achieved and discovered. Much of this is in spite of tough and difficult circumstances.

Some of the best innovations have emerged from playing around with problems—how to resolve or fix something. Similarly, many successful entrepreneurs and product innovations have emerged by thinking of new and better ways of doing things.

We might think there's nothing left to learn; it's all been invented or solved. But no, problems will always emerge and breed more problems. Creativity helps us to 'think out of the box', to apply leverage and dexterity to problem solving and solution seeking.

Being adaptable allows us to take a step to the side, to see things slightly differently and to grab a different perspective. We can take the knocks when they occur, we can change our plans or minds for the greater good. We can still retain our principles and purpose but we adapt, we evolve, we cope, we change.

Is this the same as 'tolerating ambiguity'? In a way yes. Ambiguity is the unknown, uncertain, doubt, vagueness and obscurity. We don't know stuff. And yet as we have discussed in other chapters, we resist change because we like the status quo, the certainty, the structure and the known.

Top Tips

Accept it
Developing an acceptance perspective in a range of situations can immediately give you the leverage to simply let things be.

Continuum

Consider a line with two polar opposites at each end and the bit in the middle which equates to the grey area in between. Being fixed with your views reflects these two polarities, yet often the reality is much more grey. For instance, think of an issue which has two opposing beliefs, such as politics (Labour vs Conservative, Democrat vs Republican etc.) and think of all the groups and parties which exist between or beyond them. With anything you are trying to understand there is a continuum to understand and make sense of.

Information

You can be well informed and knowledgeable about something and not have a fixed or strong opinion.

Take a chance on me

Often we want or feel we need to know finite stuff to give us clarity. But sometimes taking a risk can generate significant rewards. Get as much insight and information you can to hedge your bets and try something different or new. It doesn't have to involve money and preferably not physical risk.

Vulnerability

We don't like to feel vulnerable. But then we don't always possess a cast iron shield. If we accept a degree of managed vulnerability, then we open ourselves to greater and wider possibilities.

Structure

Having a safety net gives you the space or leverage to be adaptable and tolerate uncertainty. Assess the options and availability of structures and support which can give you the cocoon in which you can swim the sea of ambiguity.

Options

Consider the art of problem solving. You have a problem, you consider a range of solutions and you select the best one. Wading in ambiguity is a crucial part of this assessment process.

Creativity before clarity

Ask any artist if they start with a fixed outcome. Unlikely. You need the flexibility, perhaps the ambiguity, to tease out options and ideas. One thing then leads to another.

The art of learning

Whilst education systems often focus on the acquisition of knowledge, it is more helpful to develop the skills of learning. You learn by inquisitiveness, by asking questions (sometimes dumb questions) and you think of different ways of doing things. Learn to learn and you can adapt to almost anything.

Comfort zone

Step out of what is safe and familiar and you may feel uncomfortable. But you'll also notice you probably become more alert and attune to possibilities. Your brain will be sniffing out options and solutions even if your conscious awareness doesn't know it.

Action Plan 59: Dishing Out Ambiguity

Tolerating ambiguity is about working towards a solution without all the facts or the benefit of hindsight. If you were cooking my dinner tonight and you offered steak and chips, you could just take out some steaks and slap it on the grill. OR, you could ask if I wanted the steak rare, medium or well done and try to meet my expectations. Already you are finding a potential solution by tolerating ambiguity. Personally, I'd probably ask for 'medium/rare', which is my expectation and now yours. It might happen or it might not. But at the end of the day, who cares. I get a steak. That's my ambiguity and yours. It's only food. If I'm hungry it satisfies me. Job done. Ambiguity over. Thanks for the meal!

Consider a scenario where you have a task which is ambiguous or has an unclear outcome.

Name the task: _____

Why is it ambiguous? _____

Why does it matter? _____

How can you get clarity? _____

From whom? _____

What options exist for you? 1. _____

2. _____

3. _____

Potential outcomes/solutions? 1. _____

2. _____

3. _____

Visualise, accept, savour and enjoy each option, outcome and solution. You have just tolerated ambiguity.

60

Procrastination

Spotlight

This chapter has been left until the end of the book which just goes to show how common procrastination really is.

Procrastination involves delaying or postponing something which we might or could respond to sooner or earlier; we know we need to do something, but we make some judgement to delay it. If it doesn't matter or isn't important, then it's not really procrastinating because it loses relevance and timeliness. Normally it's about something that does matter. And we usually know it.

Procrastination is one of those subjects which straddles both stress management and resilience. From a stress point of view it has the potential to trigger significant anxiety and worry because it involves the inactivity of piling up tasks which can lead to overload and burnout. Even if it's not about an accumulation of uncompleted tasks, comparable stress can be accrued from a single delayed task, like the slow drip of a leaking tap. It just continues to niggle away in the background. It becomes a preoccupation that just doesn't go away. And this can take up so much angst energy.

From a resilience perspective, procrastination creates a wall or barrier to smooth and effective life management. One task persistently delayed can have a significant knock-on effect on other areas of life and put out of kilter the equilibrium of a stable life. For instance, you delay a report that should have been completed, yet you think about it on your commute home, when you're preparing your dinner, as you fail to get to sleep, as you awake at 3 in the morning, on your days off, on your way back into work and so on. What wasted energy!

Whilst procrastination can be associated with avoiding fears, worries or anxieties, it also breeds new fears, worries and anxieties. It simply moves the target, but the problem remains. What is it that stops us? What do we fear? Do we worry that we can't do the job or it won't be good enough? In most cases, it'll be more damaging to do nothing than to start or make the attempt to begin.

If we're paralysed by a fear of failure, then doing nothing means we've failed before we have even started. Game over. Or it might even be the fear of success: what if I do so well I have to take on more responsibility? OK, but what if you don't have to take on more responsibility? You have catastrophised about something which might never happen. We can choose how to deal with consequences, if they occur and when they occur.

Or is it a more practical issue of not having the right tools or resources? In which case it might be about who we can find or contact who can give us the support we need.

Often, once we start something, we have no problem, and we find that we wonder what all the fuss was in the first place. The thought of it was much worse. Taking that very first step can be crucial.

It might also be that the task we need to complete generates no interest for us whatsoever. It's one of these things that has to be done but is boring and demotivating. But that's life. Not everything's going to be stimulating or riveting stuff. We all have to get on with the mundane and maybe this helps us appreciate the more exciting projects when they emerge.

Procrastinating doesn't make something go away; it sustains the purgatory and agony of inertia and apathy.

Top Tips

Know-how
If you have a block of not knowing enough about your task or where or how to start, ask someone. Can you delegate to someone who won't have the same procrastination battle as you?

Writer's block
If you're staring at a blank screen or piece of paper and you don't know where to start, write anything: what you had for dinner last night, your last shopping experience, what you did on your holiday last year. Anything that just gets you physically tapping words on your keyboard or writing with your pen. THEN, once you are in the 'zone' you start the real stuff.

Baby steps
Plan out how to tackle a job in small steps, one at a time. This will allow you to move onto the starting blocks and take the first steps forward. Once you have momentum, maintain one step at a time and you'll finish the race on time and in time.

Make a plan
Schedule, plan and prioritise. Work out a structure which gives you clarity of what you will do when. By breaking it down into manageable parts, it will feel less daunting to start.

Feel the vibes
If you can't get started, imagine yourself smugly completing your task; how you'll feel, the relief which will flood over you, and the warm satisfaction inside. Savour, track back and start that journey.

The tough gets going
If you regard tough times as the point at which you retreat and go in a different direction, then you're always going to do this. Seek out opportunities and triumphs from the difficult times. The more you do this, the more you'll embrace adversity and challenge, and begin to relish overcoming them.

Uncertainty

We can't know everything that's going to happen in the future. The future is, by its very nature, uncertain. We can connect with the future by living in the here and now, which means engaging with and acting in the present, rather than later. This actually pulls the future into a certain present.

Break it down

Schedule your task with a beginning, middle and end and this will help you construct three mini-tasks which are already more achievable than the global task. Split each block into a further three to make it easier to start and offer a visual plan.

Biorhythms

Often carrying out the harder tasks at the start of the day is better, especially if you are feeling fresh and motivated, although it is also true that if you are most awake at the end of the day due to your biorhythms then save the harder tasks for then—but don't use this as an excuse to delay!

Prove it

How do you benefit from procrastinating, both in the current moment and in the future? What are you gaining and what are you losing?

Action Plan 60: Procrastinator Annihilator

Write out something which you are putting off or delaying:

_____

_____

_____

_____

Think hard about the disadvantages and advantages of delaying this task.
Disadvantages

1. _____
2. _____
3. _____
4. _____
5. _____

Advantages

1. _____
2. _____
3. _____
4. _____
5. _____

What does the above evidence tell you?

_____
_____
_____
_____
_____

References

de Shazer, S. (1985). *Keys to Solution in Brief Therapy*. New York: Norton.
Doran, G. T. (1981). There's a SMART Way to Write Management Goals and Objectives. *Management Review, 70*(II), 35–36.
Glasser, W. (2001). *Counselling with Choice Theory*. New York: HarperCollins.
Goleman, D. (1995). *Emotional Intelligence. Why It Can Matter More than IQ*. London: Bloomsbury.
Hayes, S. C., Strosahl, K. D., & Wilson, K. G. (1999). *Acceptance and Commitment Therapy: An Experiential Approach to Behaviour Change*. New York: Guildford Press.
Kübler-Ross, E. (1969). *On Death and Dying*. New York: Macmillan.
Maslow, A. H. (1943). A Theory of Human Motivation. *Psychological Review, 50*(4), 370–396.
Maslow, A. H. (1954). *Motivation and Personality*. New York: Harper and Row.
Rogers, C. (1980). *A Way of Being*. Boston: Houghton-Mifflin.

Index

A
Acceptance and Commitment Therapy, 261
Addiction, 209–214
Ambiguity, 12, 85, 91, 96, 145, 164, 256, 292, 333, 351–355
Anxiety, 3, 4, 35, 37, 43, 47, 61, 77, 78, 84, 85, 89, 91, 92, 100, 117, 119, 133–137, 140, 164, 182, 193, 227, 229, 233, 236, 277, 282, 297–299, 310, 311, 334, 340, 346, 357, 358

B
Bereavement, 37, 129, 130, 157–161, 200, 281, 303
Burnout
   A-B-C, 348–349
   behavioural, 346, 349
   emotional, 345, 346, 348, 349
   physical, 345, 346, 349
   psychological, 345

C
Change-focused, 333–338
Chaos, 9–12, 47, 94
Children, 175–178, 187–190, 194, 195, 199–203, 205, 257, 303, 304, 334
Choice, 6, 9–14, 29, 36, 38, 43, 50, 54, 56, 57, 60–61, 68, 71, 72, 95, 106, 124, 132, 142, 164, 166, 175–177, 181, 195, 200, 202, 206, 208, 212, 244, 245, 262, 274, 283–284, 321, 323, 336, 337
Cognitive Behavioural Therapy (CBT), 148–149
Conflict, 35, 41–46, 55, 103, 104, 125, 127, 153, 163, 166, 167,

169, 170, 178, 189, 194, 228, 244, 245, 268, 273, 328, 351
Constructive anger, 279–284
Control, 3–6, 9–14, 36, 40, 42, 48, 54, 56, 60, 102, 103, 135, 147, 158, 165, 172, 176, 194, 202, 207, 209, 217, 222, 224, 231, 235, 236, 245, 274, 280, 281, 287, 299, 303, 306, 323, 334, 346
Crisis management, 342–343
Criticism, 21–27, 84, 154, 277, 279

D

Deadline, 4, 15–18, 31, 60, 322

E

Efficiency, 29–33
Elderly, 151–155, 218, 315, 334
Emotional intelligence, 106, 256, 267–271, 348
Empathise–Apologise–Compromise (EAC), 45–46, 283

G

Goleman, Daniel, 267

K

Knowns
 known unknowns, 65, 68
 unknown unknowns, 65, 66, 68

L

Language, 22, 23, 44, 106, 111, 146, 269, 279, 287

M

Mindfulness, 95, 102, 182, 183, 297–301
Ministry of Transport (MOT), 123–128

N

Networking, 7, 72, 75, 109–113
Niebuhr, Reinhold, 261

P

Pain, 118, 119, 140, 158, 159, 182, 184, 227–231, 234, 235, 261, 262, 282, 298, 346
Perfectionism, 5, 60, 80, 83–87, 136
Pregnancy, 139, 181–185
Prioritisation, 4, 6, 15–19, 31, 101, 152, 252, 263, 322
Problem-focused, 321–325
Procrastination, 357–361
Public speaking, 77–81, 115, 134, 147

R

Reconciliation, 130–131, 178
Redundancy, 12, 47–51, 139, 339
Rejection, 21–27, 172
Relaxation, 78, 102, 136–137, 141, 147, 183, 222–223, 229–230, 309–313, 347
Retirement, 47–51, 256

S

Satisfaction, 7, 53–57, 83, 243–247, 253, 317, 359
Savviness, 105–108

Self-care, 158–159, 236, 310, 315–319
Serenity Creed, 261
Solution-focused, 11, 327–331
Stress indicator, 118, 119

Teenager, 193–197, 199
Thinking negatively, 145, 148

Visualisation, 312–313, 355

Wellness, 221–225
Work-life, 55, 101, 165, 211, 222, 249–253, 317, 347
Workload, 3–8, 59, 60

Printed by Printforce, United Kingdom